Alternative Traditions

ALTERNATIVE TRADITIONS

Sangharakshita

Windhorse Publications

Alternative Traditions

Windhorse Publications
136 Renfield Street
Glasgow G2 3AU

© Windhorse Publications 1986

Printed by F. Crowe & Sons Ltd.
11 Concorde Road
Norwich, Norfolk.

Cover illustration by Dharmachari Aloka

ISBN 0 904766 22 5

CONTENTS

DEDICATION

To the Memory of
EDWARD CONZE
(1904-1979)

Despite whose reminders
I did not review
MEMOIRS OF A MODERN GNOSTIC

Preface

To a greater extent then ever before in history, those who feel drawn to the spiritual life are in a position to decide which of the various spiritual traditions of mankind they wish to follow. Previously this was by no means the case. For one born in almost any part of Western Europe, for example, there was no choice except to follow Christianity in its Roman Catholic form. Any attempt at deviation from the dominant socio-religious orthodoxy being ruthlessly suppressed. With the coming of the Renaissance and the Reformation, however, a great change took place. The individual found himself free to choose not only between Catholicism and Protestantism but, increasingly, between this or that form of Protestantism, whether Lutheran, Calvinist, Anabaptist and so on. He even found himself free to choose between Christianity itself and the various alternative traditions which had either survived 'underground' in an attenuated form or been reconstituted from their literary remains as these happened to become available. Eventually, as contact was established with hitherto unknown parts of the world and as their spiritual traditions, too, gradually became known, the individual's scope for choice among the spiritual traditions of mankind became virtually unlimited.

Now we have a situation in which representatives of all the major religions can be found in practically every larger city of the Western world, from Buenos Aires to Vancouver and from Dublin to Istanbul. Where such representatives are not found their corresponding literature, at least, is readily available. Whether reliable or unreliable, popular or scholarly, books on both Western and Eastern (i.e. Asian), Christian and non-Christian, spiritual traditions are obtainable not only from libraries but from drugstores and railway bookstalls everywhere. One of the biggest surprises of my life occurred when, touring Greece with a friend in the summer of 1966, I found copies of Lobsang Rampa's *The Third Eye* (purportedly the autobiography of a Tibetan Buddhist lama) on display in the kiosks of even the remoter towns and villages through which we passed. Though one could have wished to see this notorious work replaced by a more authentic version of Tibetan Buddhism, it was significant that even a distant and distorted echo of the Buddha's teaching should have penetrated so far.

Buddhism in its various sectarian forms is, in fact, established as widely and as securely in Western Europe and the Americas as any of the Eastern, non-Christian spiritual traditions. Sri Lankan viharas, Vietnamese pagodas, and Tibetan gompas — even Japanese stupas — are rapidly becoming an accepted part of the urban landscape. In the same way, Buddhist classics such as the *Dhammapada*, the *Diamond Sutra*, and the *Tibetan Book of the Dead*, now regularly feature on the shelves of those having the remotest pretensions to spiritual literacy. Indeed, since the 1950s the amount of shelf space occupied by such works has increased tenfold and twentyfold. Publishers in the major Western languages, particularly English, have vied with one another in bringing out not only translations of classic Buddhist texts, both canonical and non-canonical, but also original works on every conceivable aspect of Buddhist philosophy, ethics, meditation, art, literature, history, economics, anthropology, and sociology.

As a result, books on Buddhism are now available in

comparatively large numbers — even if, in some cases, at a price only the rich can afford. These books fall into a number of categories. There are books written (or translated) by Buddhists, whether Eastern or Western, and books written by non-Buddhists. There are popular books and scholarly books, books written from an ecumenical and books written from a sectarian point of view, books based on a profound and books based on a superficial knowledge of Buddhism. Above all, perhaps, there are reliable and unreliable books on Buddhism, that is to say, books in which the fundamentals of Buddhism are reflected with comparative fidelity and those in which they suffer more or less serious distortion.

In these circumstances it becomes necessary to discriminate. As the number of books issuing from the publishing houses of the Western world increases with every year that goes by, we have to view them with a more and more genuinely critical eye. Gone are the days — days which personally I can well remember — when a new book on Buddhism was a phenomenon of such rarity that, on its appearance, it could be hailed with delight and read with avidity almost regardless of its merits. Whether a casual or a serious, an old or a new student of Buddhism, we now have to separate the wheat from the chaff or, in more Buddhistic phrase, the sound from the rotten timber. We have to distinguish between what truly belongs, and what does not belong, to that great raft on which untold thousands of sentient beings have been, are being, and will be ferried across the ocean of birth-and-death to the Other Shore of Nirvana or Perfect Enlightenment.

This is what I have tried to do in the following pages, both for my own benefit and for the benefit of others. As each new book on Buddhism appeared (and hundreds must have arrived on my desk in the course of the last decade) I sought to ascertain to what extent it was a product of a genuine understanding of the spirit and the letter of the Buddha's teaching and what bearing it had on the actual practice of the Dharma, especially here in the West. From time to time, as I came across errors that needed to be exposed, or insights that it seemed desirable to underline, or simply as I felt that a certain book was deserving of a wider circle of readers, I committed my thoughts to paper in the form of a review article.

These reviews (and I would have written more of them if I had had more time), together with a much smaller number of reviews of books which, though not dealing with Buddhism, were of interest from a (Western) Buddhist point of view, made their appearance in the quarterly *FWBO Newsletter* between the years 1974 and 1980. In preparing them for publication in their present form it was originally my intention to arrange them in chronological order. On second thoughts, however, I decided to organize them into three main groups, according to whether the works of which they were reviews dealt with the Theravada, with Ch'an or Zen, or with Tibetan Buddhism, which between them represent the three principle phases in the historical development of Indian Buddhism, i.e. the Hinayana, the Mahayana, and the Vajrayana. Before the first of these groups I placed the reviews of those works which related to the general spiritual situation in the West, or to the background of Indian philosophy and religion against which Buddhism itself arose, while after the last group I placed a review and an article in which the life and work of two of the greatest English writers are examined from a Buddhist point of view.

Thus the book begins by plunging into the alternative traditions of the West. In a review whose heading gives its title to the whole work, I take a quick look at the history of communes and intentional communities in the West, from the earliest times down to the present century, as well as at the 'heresy' of the Cathars or Albigenses and at Gnosticism. This gives me an opportunity of stressing the difference between the commune and the intentional community (or between the 'positive group' and the spiritual community, as we say in the FWBO), as well as of correcting a dangerous misunderstanding with regard to the nature of Buddhist meditation. I then consider the theses of two representatives of Christian socio-religious orthodoxy, one of whom tries to meet the challenge of the various alternative Eastern traditions by arguing that a 'passing over' into another religion is followed by an equal and opposite 'coming back' to one's 'own' religion. Having pointed out that some of Christianity's 'prodigal sons' have in fact gone for good, I turn to a highly idiosyncratic cross-cultural critique of modern 'mystical movements' and, in 'Hedonism and the Spiritual Life', attempt a Buddhist critique of that critique. This involves a discussion of such topics as the nature of the mystical experience, the place of the pleasure-principle in the spiritual life, the difference between *śamathā* or calm and *vipásyanā* or insight, and the difference between puritanism and asceticism. Since the discussion is conducted in both Buddhist and Hindu terms we have, in effect, passed from the alternative traditions of the West not only to what, from the Western point of view, are the alternative traditions of the East, but also to the philosophical and religious background of Buddhism. This introductory group of reviews therefore concludes with an examination of the different Indian traditions of *ahiṃsā* or non-violence, both Vedic and non-Vedic, and an inquiry into the relation between the practice of Yoga — in the broader sense — and the study of Indian philosophy. I also take exception to an implied disparagement of poetry.

During the time that I was writing the reviews that make up the present volume, not many books on the Theravada appeared. The first main group of reviews therefore consists of only a single item, though this review is one of the longest in the book and deals, moreover, with a subject of considerable theoretical and practical importance. That subject is the development of Sinhalese religio-nationalism. It was a development that began early. Commenting chapter by chapter on a work written by a Sinhalese 'political bhikkhu' turned scholar, I see how from the 3rd century BCE Buddhism gradually degenerated from a universal into an ethnic religion and the Sangha from a spiritual community into a cultural elite. In the course of this process Buddhism becomes (in the ex-political bhikkhu's own words) 'an institution of the Sinhalese monarchy', Sri Lanka (Ceylon) becomes the Buddha's own country, the killing of non-Buddhists is declared to be no sin, and monks, having decided that scholarship is more important than spiritual practice, proceed to acquire wealth and political power. It is indeed a shameful and shocking story, and the quondam political Bhikkhu tells it with a complacency, and even pride, on which I more than once remark. I also try to clear up his confused and muddled thinking on such topics as Buddhism and social service, the 'renunciation' of Nirvana, the Bodhisattva ideal, the condition of the people of India at the time of the Buddha, and what makes one a Buddhist. Re-reading this review after an interval of eleven years, in the light of the tragic events that have now brought the people of Sri Lanka to the brink of civil war, it is more obvious to me than ever where the origins of that increasingly bloody conflict are to be found. I earnestly hope that the political bhikkus of Sri Lanka and their lay supporters will see the error of their ways before it is too late.

From Sinhalese religio-nationalism I turn with relief to Mahayana Buddhism and, in particular, to Ch'an or Zen.

After welcoming the appearance of the first volume of an important new translation of the *White Lotus Sutra* (and incidentally laying down four conditions that must be fulfilled before this sutra can be fully known and appreciated in the West), in the second main group of reviews I direct my attention to seven works on what was, for a number of years, the most popular form of Buddhism in the West. Some of these works are translations of classics that have moulded the spiritual life of generations of Far Eastern Buddhists, while others are original productions by modern 'authorities' on Zen, both oriental and occidental. In the case of the former I find myself able to do little more than utter cries of admiration, so great are the spiritual riches to which the worthy translators have given us access. In the case of the latter, however, the cries are more often cries of outrage than of admiration, and I am obliged to devote much of my space to pointing out that Zen anecdotes should not be read out of context, that 'Daily Life Practice' is not the same thing as acceptance of the status quo, that words and concepts must be distinguished from realities, that mouth Zen is not heart Zen, that Zen practice does have something to do with Buddhist philosophy, and so on.

Tibetan Buddhism being probably the richest form of Buddhism, it is not surprising that the eight works with which I concern myself in the third main group of reviews should between them cover a wider field than those on Ch'an or Zen. Like the latter they comprise both translations of classics and original works by authorities in whose case single inverted commas are definitely *not* required. I begin by taking a fairly close look at three translations, one from Tibetan, one from Sanskrit via Tibetan, and one from Tibetan but of a text closely modelled on Sanskrit sources — a fact that indicates the complexity of modern Buddhist studies. In doing so I draw attention to the importance Tibetan Buddhism attaches to the power of reasoning, even in the case of special meditation practices of the Highest Yoga (Anuttara-yoga) of the Tantrayana, and dwell on the strictly practical nature of the Abhidharma tradition of psychological analysis. I also deplore a Western Buddhist scholar's immersion in his own self-contained world of idiosyncratic renderings of standard Buddhist terms. Having done this, I direct my attention to an important new overview of the Tibetan religious world and to a short account of the spread of 'Lamaism' in Mongolia, both of which stress the importance of political and economic factors. In between, I glance at the autobiography of a contemporary Gelugpa monk, the nobility and disinterestedness of whose life greatly impresses me, but whom I strongly suspect of having been the victim of intellectual cramming. The third main group of reviews concludes with an appreciation of the marvellous life of the Great Guru Padmasambhava, the virtual founder of Tibetan Buddhism, as described in the beautifully produced translation of one of the most vivid and colourful products of the Tibetan imagination, and a much shorter appreciation of an anthology of translations from Tibetan Buddhist literature.

The last group of reviews is of a rather miscellaneous character. After pointing out, in connection with two small but useful publications, that just as Buddhist art is visual Dharma so Buddhist instrumental music and chanting is, in reality, aural Dharma, I examine two collections of essays by one of the most distinguished Buddhist scholars of our day (since deceased). This brings me to a review of an illustrated biography of one great English writer and an article on the life and work of another. In the first I confine myself to a single topic, that of the failure of a celebrated modern attempt to establish a spiritual community, and try to indentify the causes of that failure in the light of our own experience of spiritual community within the FWBO. This leads me to enumerate four basic principles. In the article which concludes this group of reviews, and thus marks the end of the present volume, I am concerned not with a single topic but with the whole life and work of my second great English writer insofar as this already communicates something of the spirit of Buddhism in the language of Western culture. Bringing Buddhism into contact with writers of this sort will, I aver, hasten its aquisition of that language and thus facilitate the spread of Buddhism in the West.

Thus the wheel comes full circle. From the alternative traditions of the West we have passed to the alternative traditions of the East, as represented especially by Buddhism, and from a Buddhism communicated in the language — or languages — of Eastern culture to the possibility, at least, of a Buddhism communicated in the language of Western culture. As we have done this, and as we have cast a critical but not unfriendly eye over a small but fairly comprehensive selection of books on Buddhism and on topics of interest to Western Buddhists, I hope I have been able to discriminate between what is in conformity with the Dharma and what is not, thereby contributing to the establishment not only of Western Buddhism, but of a purified and renascent Buddhism throughout the world.

Alternative Traditions*

Many people, dissatisfied with the present state of Western civilization and their own way of life, are looking for a viable alternative. Some turn to the philosophies and spiritual traditions of the East, hoping that they may find what they are looking for there. Others explore Western civilization itself, taking a second look at the various philosophies and spiritual traditions which, from time to time, threatened the dominant socio-religious 'orthodoxy' and were either completely destroyed by it or survived only in peripheral or subterranean forms. Kenneth Rexroth, Arthur Guirdham, and Jacques Lacarrière all look for their alternative in the West, though Rexroth's interest in Zen is well known, and it is no coincidence, perhaps, that their books should all come to our notice at the same time. It is no coincidence either, perhaps, that although based on wide reading all three books should be popular rather than scholarly in character — one, indeed, a best-seller in the original French. Although concerned with what is broadly the same field, the field of 'alternative traditions' of the West, the American poet-critic, the

---

*Kenneth Rexroth *Communalism: From its Origins to the Twentieth Century.* (London: Peter Owen, 1975)

Arthur Guirdham *The Great Heresy* (Jersey: Neville Spearman, 1977)

Jacques Lacarrière *The Gnostics* Foreword by Lawrence Durrell. Translated from the French by Nina Rootes (London: Peter Owen, 1977)

English psychiatrist, and the French poet and wanderer, are all concerned with it in different ways, or at different levels. Kenneth Rexroth explores alternative forms of socio-economic organization, Arthur Guirdham what was once virtually an alternative religion, and Jacques Lacarrière an alternative philosophy. Even for those who, like ourselves, look to the East rather than to the West for our basic inspiration, all three books are of considerable interest and value.

By communalism Kenneth Rexroth means the theory of those who believe in libertarian communism and who are members of intentional communities, usually but by no means always religious in inspiration. Like all 'communists', such people want to abolish the State and return society to an organic community of non-coercive human relations. *Communalism* tells how successful, or how unsuccessful, some of them were in doing this. It is a study of the history of communes and intentional communities, mainly Western, from their known beginnings to the twentieth century. Leaving aside palaeolithic hunting groups and the neolithic village, as well as the Essenes and similar groups, the communities described fall mainly into three categories. First, there are the monastic and semi-monastic communities of the Dark Ages and the Middle Ages, whether 'orthodox' like the Benedictines and the Cistercians, or 'heterodox' like the Waldenses, the Brethren of the Free Spirit, and the Taborites. Next, there are the various radical Reformation groups, some pacifist as well as communist, the most important being the Central European Anabaptists, Mennonites, and Hutterites, and the English Diggers. Finally there are the American communes and intentional communities, beginning with groups of European origin like the Ephratans, the Harmonists or Rappists, and the Separatists, and eventually including not only Amana and the Shakers, but secular communities like New Harmony and the Fourierist phalansteries, as well as experiments like Brook Farm and Oneida, and the transplanted, and immensely successful, Hutterites.

As one goes through this enthralling study, following the fortunes of communalism over a period of more than a thousand years, one is struck not only by the abundance and diversity of the groups and movements involved, but also by the amount of human energy that went into the search for an alternative form of socio-economic organization. The picture that presents itself is of wave after wave surging up from the depths of Western society and dashing against the bastions of the established order. Sometimes a breach is made, and the waters pour in, flooding the low-lying areas and forming, here and there, little pools that may last for centuries. More often, the wave is repulsed, and falls back baffled into the sea. Since early man went through a long stage of primitive communism, it is as though people had an inbuilt tendency to revert to a communal way of living whenever possible, particularly in times of crisis. 'Whenever the power structure falters, the general tendency is to replace it with free communism' (p. xviii). This applies to power structures of every kind, 'Communist' as well as capitalist. One is also struck, going through this study, by the extreme adaptability of human nature. There seems to be no limit to the extent to which quite ordinary people are prepared to give up long-cherished attitudes and accept major changes in every aspect of their lives. Order or disorder, austerity or self-indulgence, strict celibacy or complete promiscuity, — all are equally welcome provided they result in an ultimately more satisfying life for those concerned. What perhaps strikes one most in the history of communalism, however, is the violent hostility with which groups and movements of a communalist nature were regarded by the official

Church, Lutheran as well as Catholic. Originally, of course, groups and movements of this sort, many of which had the avowed aim of reviving the communalism of primitive Christianity, could be incorporated within the existing order in the form of monastic communities. Rexroth in fact seems to think that monasticism was the Church's way of 'containing' libertarian communism and preventing it spreading through the rest of society. Be that as it may, when it could no longer be contained in this manner, and when communalist groups and movements started attacking the existing order of things, denouncing the Church for its manifold corruptions and denying the efficacy of the sacraments when administered by unworthy hands — even denying that sacraments and priests are necessary to salvation at all, thus striking at the very root of the Church's power — then the Church fell upon them with fire and sword and exterminated them without mercy wherever it found them.

From a study of this kind there is clearly much to be learned, and in the Epilogue Kenneth Rexroth helps us by drawing a few conclusions of his own. Secular communes, he assures us, have almost always failed in very short order. 'A simple belief that all men are brothers is not sufficiently well defined to inspire a strong commitment' (p. 295). The longest-lived colonies owed their cohesion and commitment to supernatural sanctions, besides being governed by individuals of powerful charisma. In more Buddhistic terms, the longest-lived colonies were spiritual communities, and recognized some kind of spiritual heirarchy, in however rudimentary a form. Ceremonies and the practice of confession are also factors making for cohesion, as well as a certain degree of interpersonal tension. Communism as such does not seem to have been a factor in the failure of most colonies, though many of those that fail, perhaps the majority, do so for economic reasons. On the contrary, 'Wherever there existed powerful forces for commitment and cohesion, a carefully screened membership, and intelligent leaders with wide practical experience, communism proved to be, economically, extremely successful' (p. 297). Rexroth also emphasizes that communal living (he is referring, of course, to 'mixed' communities) is in theory very advantageous to women, for most of the work of a housewife or mother can then be divided and distributed, so that each woman has considerable leisure. Summing up, he says that in all the many books which have been written about the communalist movement in America in the nineteenth century, there is little disagreement as to the factors that make for success. They are: 'A religion, or at least a powerful ideology which all the members of the group accept, which should include the belief that the dominant society fails to provide sufficient value for a happy life, and is sick, or doomed, or dying, or, nowadays, already dead, and that the commune is a saving remnant plucked from burning' (p. 301). In addition the community needs a leader with powerful charisma, the ability to persuade people, equanimity, and a wide range of talents. There should also be an accepted method of assigning and rotating tasks, with both sexes sharing the boring jobs and housekeeping. On the negative side, a community cannot survive as such with a completely 'open gate' policy. 'Selectivity is the first law of communalism . . . The communes that are most successful today either do not allow visitors at all, or do not allow them to stay more than overnight, and prospective members are subjected to a searching novitiate' (p. 304).

In all this there is very little from which a Buddhist need dissent. The conclusions Kenneth rexroth draws undoubtedly do follow from the histories of the groups he surveys, and to the extent of their applicability are valid for communes and intentional communities of all kinds. This is not to say that his study does not have its limitations, especially on the theoretical side. The most serious of these is that he does not make sufficiently clear the distinction between commune and intentional community, or as we would say, between the 'positive group' and the spiritual community. This is because he does not recognize the importance of the principle of individuality, or see that whereas the group is of a collective and corporate nature a spiritual community is a free association of true individuals, i.e. of those who have developed self-awareness and emancipated themselves at least from the cruder forms of group conditioning.* Because he fails to recognize the importance of individuality, and therefore to distinguish commune from intentional community, he tends, at times, to see the spread of communalism in terms of a sort of mass movement. To the extent that communalism means communes, i.e. the positive group, the spread of communalism may indeed be a mass movement (some chapters of his study demonstrate as much), but to speak of the spread of intentional communities in this way involves a contradiction in terms. Failure to appreciate the importance of individuality has other consequences. As we have already noted, Rexroth tends to see communalism as a reversion to the primitive communism of early man, in other words as a sort of sociological throwback. Again, this may well be true of libertarian communism as such, but it is not true of the spiritual community. The latter may indeed incorporate elements from an earlier form of social organization, but inasmuch as it consists of a free association of true individuals it is essentially not a regression but a higher 'evolutionary' development. There are also limitations that

*For further elucidation see my tape-recorded lecture on 'The Individual, the Group, and the Community'.

relate to monasticism. Besides seeing organized
monasticism as 'a method of quarantining the Christian
life' (p. 30), and celibacy as a device for preventing (lay)
monasticism from becoming a counter-culture, Kenneth
Rexroth gives the impression that monasticism dropped
out of the picture somewhere about the time of the
Reformation, whereas the truth of the matter is that, both
in East and West, the longest lived of all intentional
communities are monastic communities. Indeed, the
monastic community has claims to be considered the
spiritual community *par excellence*. Despite its limitations,
however, which are limitations of perspective and interpretation rather than of informational content, and as such
easily remedied, *Communalism* is required reading for all
who are engaged in the creation of a truly alternative
society. Though there are specialist studies of a number of
the groups that Kenneth Rexroth describes, I doubt if there
is any other book that discusses so many of them in such
detail, or that paints such a vivid and inspiring picture of a
movement which, despite all the setbacks it has
experienced, remains the only real hope of mankind.

The 'heresy' of Dr Guirdham's title is that of the Cathars
or Albigenses, who are only briefly mentioned by Kenneth
Rexroth (pp. 36-37). Strictly speaking, Catharism was not
so much a heresy as the latest manifestation of an entirely
different religious and philosophical tradition, a tradition
which tended to assume a Christian form in Europe, just
as it tended to assume a Zoroastrian form in Persia and a
Buddhistic form in Central Asia and China. The Cathars
indeed considered themselves the true Christians, and
their Church the true Church, and to the extent that
Christianity itself was of Gnostic rather than Judaic origin
they may well have been right. To the people of Languedoc
they were simply the *Bonshommes* (good men). The ancient

tradition of which Catharism was the latest manifestation was that of Dualism. According to Arthur Guirdham, its basic tenets were threefold. It believed that forces of good and evil existed in the universe from the beginning and would do so to the end; that the world was created not by God but by the Devil, who was identical with the Old Testament Jehovah, and that man was a spiritual being distinct from matter who in course of successive 'rein-carnations' purified himself by leading a moral and spiritual life until he was reunited with the Light. The Cathars denied the efficacy of the sacraments. They refused to believe that sins could be wiped out by means of divine grace, or that this grace could be dispensed through the official sacramental channels by the priests of the established (Catholic) Church solely by virtue of their ordination, regardless of their moral and spiritual character. The Cathar community comprised two kinds of followers. There were the Perfect, or Cathars proper, and the Believers. The Perfect, both men and women, practised absolute non-violence and chastity, and abstained from the eating of meat. The Believers, who formed the majority, while fully accepting the basic tenets of Catharism were less rigorous in practice. Catharism spread to Western Europe probably from what is now part of Yugoslavia and Bulgaria. It appeared in southern France at least as early as the beginning of the eleventh century and towards the end of the twelfth century was well established there, being particularly strong in Languedoc and the county of Provence, which then formed one of the most prosperous and highly civilized areas in the whole of Europe. In Languedoc it was indeed the dominant religion, being supported by all classes of people. (It was from Albi, a town in Languedoc, that the Cathars received the name by which they are best known. The term Cathar itself means 'Pure'.) The established Church became thoroughly alarmed. Earlier attempts to suppress Catharism having failed, in 1207 Pope Innocent III launched what has become infamous in history as the Albigensian Crusade. The loot-hungry nobles of northern France were called upon to crush the heresy by force of arms, and offered remission of all their sins for doing so. The crusade lasted off and on for forty years. Hundreds of towns and villages were laid waste, and many tens of thousands of men, women, and children were massacred. The civilization of Languedoc was destroyed, and the whole area so badly devastated that the effects persist, it is said, down to the present day. Upwards of a thousand Perfect were burned at the stake. Catharism never recovered from the blow. In the wake of the horrors of the crusade came the terrors of the Inquisition, and by the middle of the fourteenth century Catharism as such had ceased to exist.

Not content with exterminating Catharism physically, for the last seven hundred years the Catholic Church has systematically vilified and misrepresented it. An abridged edition of M. L. Cozens's *A Handbook of Heresies*, published by Sheed and Ward in its popular 'Prayer and Practice' series as late as 1974, describes Catharism as 'poison' and accuses the Cathars of 'endeavouring by force of arms to uproot Christianity in southern France'!! (p. 63). But now the tide is turning. The literature devoted to Catharism has increased enormously during the last thirty years, and the truth about the Cathars is beginning to be known. Most of this literature is in French, and Dr Guirdham's publishers rightly claim that a book in English on the Cathars is long overdue. Part One of *The Great Heresy* deals with Catharism as it is known to historians, theologians, and philosophers. Packing a great deal of information into fourteen short chapters, Dr Guirdham describes the origins of Catharism, its brief flowering, and its terrible end, and gives a clear, fair-minded, and sensible account of its beliefs and practices. In so doing he not only 'reveals truth' but 'exposes error'. He is particularly good, in fact, at showing the complete falsity of such charges as that Catharism was pessimistic, that it advocated mass suicide, that its attitude to sex 'was at its worst perverted and at its best so ascetic as to amount to psychological self-mutilation' (p. 28), and that its followers were the enemies of society. Such misrepresentations, glibly repeated by generation after generation of historians, both Catholic and Protestant, were often based (he reminds us) on isolated statements obtained from ordinary Believers under torture. To rely for solid unbiased information about the Cathars on the registers of the Inquisition is indeed 'comparable to insisting that the Gestapo is the best authority to enlighten us as to the nature and practice of Jewry' (p. 24). The parallel between the Catholic Inquisition and the Nazi Gestapo is quite striking. 'Heretics were often condemned to wear a yellow cross, the dimensions of which were carefully stipulated, sewn on to the garments of the victim. The Nazis adopted an identical measure against the Jews' (p. 72). On balance, however, the worse of the two was the Inquisition, which 'developed into a systemized instrument of terror unequalled in human history. Over a huge area those innocent of heresy were as liable to suffer as those addicted to it. What it aimed at was the creation of an atmosphere in which Catharism simply could not live. That the latter lasted even as long as it did is proof of the toughness of its adherents. It is undeniable that the havoc wrought by the Inquisition far exceeds that achieved by the Ogpu and the Gestapo. The Jews and Poles were not wholly exterminated either actually or politically. In just short of a century Catharism, which had threatened the very existence of Catholicism in the Midi, had been reduced to a handful of clandestine activists. When one considers that Hitler had at his command all the devices for the dissemination of information and defamatory propaganda, the achievements of the Inquisition are truly impressive' (p. 75). If society had any enemies in the thirteenth century it was not the Cathars. The Cathars, far from being the anti-human monsters that they were made out to be, were in fact friends and benefactors of humanity. In particular, they sought to remove from people the insidious, soul-destroying fear of hell that, then as now, the Catholic Church so sedulously inculcated. This, Arthur Guirdham says, was perhaps the Cathars' 'most significant contribution to the welfare of the common man' (p. 23). As for their being against marriage — in Catholic eyes a most heinous offence — they were hostile to it not as an institution but as a sacrament. 'They did not believe that sexual conduct was sinful and taboo until the hour of wedlock and that afterwards what was illicit and sordid became in some way sanctified' (p.26). Had Catharism indeed been against the institution of marriage and (according to the Catholic Church) therefore against the family and society, it is difficult to see how it could have enjoyed the strong support of the Languedoc aristocracy. As Dr Guirdham remarks, 'It is not in the nature of ruling classes to plan their own destruction in full, waking consciousness' (p. 29). In view of these and other considerations he therefore concludes that Catharism was not only 'a comprehensive and lucid philosophy' (p. 26) but also 'sane and evolutionary' and even — for what the compliment is worth — 'contemporary'.

Part Two of the book deals not with Catharism as it is known to historians, theologians, and philosophers, but with its deeper teachings as revealed to the author by a group of discarnate entities, all but one of whom were alive in the twentieth century. Basing himself on these teachings, Arthur Guirdham deals, in the course of seven short chapters, with such topics as the Transmigration of

Souls, Auras, The Creation, Jewels, The Sun and the Moon, Mechanism of Evil, and Alchemy. Even those who believe in life after death and in 'reincarnation' would probably prefer, pending further investigation, to consider the material contained in this section of *The Great Heresy* strictly on its own merits. One idea that I personally found very appealing — and quite in accordance with Buddhist teaching — was that flowers develop a 'soul' as a result of the attention paid to them by human beings, and that colour and perfume are the means by which they attract this attention.

Himself a spiritist as well as a believer in reincarnation, Dr Guirdham tends to regard Catharism as having its roots in primitive Christianity — which he describes as 'a markedly spiritist religion' (p. 102) — and Christianity itself as 'an episode in the history of Dualism' (p. 103). No one reading *The Great Heresy* with even a smattering of Buddhist knowledge could fail to notice a resemblance between Catharism and Buddhism or to wonder, perhaps, if Catharism had roots in Buddhism too. Dr Guirdham is not unaware of this. He acknowledges that the likeness between the practice of Catharism and Buddhism must attract attention, and that vegetarianism and non-violence are common to both. At the same time, he is unable to agree with the late Maurice Magre, a devotee of Catharism, that the Cathars are 'the Buddhists of Europe'. According to him this is a completely erroneous over-simplification. The philosophy of Catharism, he says, is quite distinct from that of Buddhism. Whether this is indeed the case can be decided only when we have a better knowledge of Catharist philosophy — as well, perhaps, as a better knowledge of Buddhist philosophy. (It is interesting that Dr Guirdham tells us, earlier on (p. 48), that the Cathars believed, as much as the oriental philosophers who provided the bedrock of Hinduism and Buddhism, in 'the necessity of ultimately transcending the world of irreconcilable opposites'.) Meanwhile, M. Magre's statement can be taken as true at least sociologically. After all, what he said was that the Cathars were the Buddhists of Europe, i.e. that they occupied analogous positions in their respective socio-religious contexts, not that the philosophies of Catharism and Buddhism were identical. Within their widely differing time scales, the fortunes of the Cathars of southern France and the Buddhists of India, at least, were in some respects remarkably similar. One must also join issue with Arthur Guirdham on the subject of meditation. He appears to think that meditation involves emptying the mind, and that, when this is done too precipitately, it results in the mind being invaded by lower entities (p. 46). This is certainly not true of Buddhist meditation. Far from involving any emptying of the mind, Buddhist meditation involves the intensive development of skilful mental states. Nevertheless, despite misunderstandings of this sort, from what Dr Guirdham has to tell us about them in *The Great Heresy* it is clear that the beliefs and practices of the Cathars are highly relevant to Western Buddhists. (Those concerned with what the FWBO calls 'team-based right livelihood' will be interested to learn that the Cathars were 'ferocious workers' and that they had workshops in which men were trained in various cottage industries.) Even more relevant than the beliefs and practices of the Cathars is their history. At a time when, in this country, non-Christians have been suddenly made aware that they do not have quite as much freedom as they had thought, it would be well for English Buddhists at least to remind themselves that the ghosts of Pope Innocent III and the Inquisitors are still very much abroad and that it is still possible for a religion to be destroyed.

Gnosticism is not an alternative tradition of the West in

quite the same way as communalism, or even Catharism. Flourishing as it did throughout the second and third centuries in the lands all round the eastern end of the Mediterranean, it was an alternative tradition once, at least in places like Rome and Marseilles, but ceased to be such as soon as Christianity became the official religion of the Roman Empire in the fourth century. Thereafter it was subject to intense persecution and except as an underground influence survived, in the West, only in remote corners of the Balkans, where for the rest of the millenium it gathered strength for its journey to north Italy and southern France in the form of Catharism. For fifteen hundred years the West had no knowledge of groups like the Ophites and the Carpocratians, or thinkers like Basilides and Valentinus, other than what could be derived from the meagre scraps of information contained in the writings of such Fathers of the Church as Hippolytus, Irenaeus, and Eusebius, all of whom were of course interested in showing Gnosticism in the worst possible light. The position with regard to Gnosticism was, in fact, remarkably similar to that with regard to Catharism, our knowledge of which was dependent for five hundred years on the records of the Inquisition. Only with the discovery of the Askew Codex (containing the 'Pistis Sophia') towards the end of the eighteenth and of the Bruce and Berlin Codices towards the end of the nineteenth century, and above all the discovery of a complete Gnostic library at Nag Hamadi in Egypt (the ancient Chenaboskion) in about 1945, has the situation changed — and changed radically. For the first time in fifteen hundred years we know enough about Gnosticism for it to be a genuine option for some at least of those people in the West who are looking for an alternative philosophy, and the appearance of Jacques Lacarrière's 'strange and original essay', as Lawrence Durrell calls The Gnostics, is one of the signs of this changed state of affairs. All the more is it such a sign, indeed, for being — as Durrell goes on to say — 'more a work of literature than of scholarship' and 'as convincing a reconstruction of the way the Gnostics lived and thought as D. H. Lawrence's intuitive recreation of the vanished Etruscans' (p. 7).

Despite the fact that it was not a genuine option for so many centuries, Gnosticism is in principle the alternative philosophy — and religion — *par excellence.* An alternative philosophy, or an alternative way of life, is such only to the extent that it is an alternative to something else which it rejects. Gnosticism parallels Buddhism in being alternative not just to some other philosophy or religion existing beside it in the world but to 'the world' or 'conditioned existence' itself. As the irredeemable product of primeval error the world is radically evil, and man — who does not really belong to the world — should have nothing to do with it. Man is in his essence an alternative being, and for an alternative being the only appropriate philosophy — the only appropriate way of life — is one which is likewise 'alternative'. Being an alternative philosophy — an alternative wisdom, a counter-wisdom — *in principle,* and not simply by reason of its forcible suppression by official Christianity, Gnosticism was an alternative philosophy from the very beginning. Describing the doctrine of Simon Magus, Lacarriére says that here in 'the very first years of our era' we find set out the fundamental certitudes of Gnosticism, which are that 'the world we live in was not created by the true God, it is the work of an imposter, and man's task will consist in rejecting the swindle of the world, together with the Biblical and Christian teaching which claims to uphold it and all the institutions through which it is perpetuated. Thus, from the start,' he concludes, 'the Gnostic identifies himself as a marginal creature, forced (by the historical evolution of society as well as by his own inclinations) to form alternative and secret communities which will transmit the teaching' (pp. 49-50). Consequent on Gnosticism's certitude about the world is its certitude about man. Because his task is to reject the world, and because he is a marginal creature, 'man is called upon, in this struggle against the generalized oppressiveness of the real, *to create a soul for himself*, or if you prefer, to nourish, fortify, and enrich the luminous spark he carries in his inmost being' (p. 50). There are different ways of doing this. One is by means of what Lacarriére calls an *'inversion of values and symbols'* — italicizing the words to emphasize the importance of the process. This process of inversion, or 'mechanism' as he terms it, which was an aspect of the counter-life led by the Gnostics, 'tended to favour, to invest with power, light, and efficacy all those whom the orthodox tradition looks upon as the damned: Seth, the Serpent, Cain. It is these first Rebels in the history of the world whom the Gnostics were to raise to the highest dignity, to claim as the authors of their esoteric books. Their *mythical history thus transmutes itself into a counter-history which places the great rebels in the foreground'* (p. 85). Inversion of values and symbols is of course a form of deconditioning, and without deconditioning there is no creation of a soul. 'As I write this word, *deconditioning,'* Jacques Lacarrière says, 'I perceive that I am reaching the very heart of Gnostic doctrine. No knowledge, no serious contemplation, no valid choice is possible until man has shaken himself free of everything that effects his conditioning, at every level of his existence' (p. 97).

The Gnostic techniques for deconditioning oneself are of both the ascetic and the licentious type, some groups favouring the one and some the other. (Those who are *not* concerned with team-based right livelihood may be interested to find Bishop Timothy saying of the Enchites or

Messalians, one of the licentious groups, sometimes called the Lazy Men, 'They spend their time doing nothing and sleeping'.) Whether ascetic or licentious, the 'single, solitary purpose' of all techniques, of all these 'violations of all the rules and conventions', was 'to be the brutal and radical means of stripping man of his mental and bodily habits, awakening in him his sleeping being and shaking off the alienating torpor of the soul' (p. 98). Adding that he finds it strange that all the books written about Gnosticism leave their authors untouched (one could say the same thing of many books written about Buddhism), and that he is well aware that one never writes a book that is not about oneself, Jacques Lacarrière wonders why he is particularly attached to those that are known as the licentious Gnostics, that after all represent only one sect among others. 'Am I the unwitting victim of a phenomenon born in my own time,' he asks, 'one which leads us to interrogate ourselves more deeply than ever before on sexual questions?' (p. 98). Or are there other explanations? He finds it difficult to make up his mind. There is little doubt, though, that Lacarrière is a product of the century of Artaud and Sartre, and that his reading of Gnosticism is the result, to some extent, of his French literary inheritance. He sees the general Gnostic attitude towards the world as one of 'decadence', and although, formally speaking, his definition of decadence is unexceptionable, the word cannot but carry with it a *fin de siècle* flavour hardly in keeping with what Durrell calls 'the grand poetic challenge of the Gnostics' (p. 7). He also indulges in occasional outbursts of lyricism on the subject of woman, her body, and her indispensability to salvation (i.e. men's salvation). His particular conditioning shows itself most clearly, perhaps, in his failure to appreciate the importance of schools and communities, the formation of which he sees as somehow contrary to the spirit of Gnosticism. He appreciates that man is 'a stranger here'. Indeed, he devotes a whole chapter to the topic. With considerable eloquence he speaks of the Gnostics as 'the autochthons of another world', and describes 'their feeling of having fallen onto our earth like inhabitants from a distant planet, of having strayed into the wrong galaxy, and their longing to regain their true cosmic homeland, the luminous hyper-world that shimmers beyond the great nocturnal barrier' (p. 30). That 'I am *in* the world but not *of* the world', he says, is the most basic Gnostic formula. What he does not appreciate is that when one stranger, one foreigner, one Gnostic, happens to meet another he experiences not only a great relief but a great joy, and that it is out of this joy that the spiritual community is born. Because he fails to appreciate the significance of the spiritual community — indeed, seems not to believe in communities at all, or in the Oriental religions and philosophies to which, he says, those who reject the world in its modern form almost always have correlative recourse — Lacarrière seeks to discover what he calls a New Gnosticism in the pages of contemporary writers like Emile Coiran, whose works, he believes, 'match the loftiest flashes of Gnostic thought' (p. 127). But flashes, however lofty, are not enough. Literary attitudes, however striking, — literary reconstructions, however convincing, — are not enough. We need not only an alternative philosophy but an alternative religion and an alternative way of life: we need an alternative form of social organization. Perhaps Jacques Lacarrière should read Kenneth Rexroth and Arthur Guirdham — and vice versa. Perhaps all three should pay greater attention to the spiritual traditions of the East.

Calling Home the Prodigal Son*

Both these books are written by Christian academics, and both have a thesis to propound. Indeed, despite their origin on different sides of the Atlantic the non-Christian critic may be forgiven for seeing both of them as part of a defensive-offensive rearguard action waged by a traditional Christianity uneasily surviving in a post-Christian society.

Daniel Jenkins is a British, more specifically a Welsh, Presbyterian, and was until recently Chaplain and Reader at the University of Sussex and Visiting Professor at the University of London. His thesis is that the malaise of communal life in modern Britain calls for a fresh look at ourselves and our institutions, and that such a look reveals that our national consciousness and our religious heritage are more closely related than it has been customary to suppose. This is true not only of Britain as a whole, but also, more particularly, of the constituent nations of Britain, i.e. the English, the Scots, and the Welsh. Any attempt to restore the vision of Britain must therefore take into account the fact that church loyalty and national loyalty are closely linked, and that the problems of national identity in relation to Christian faith cannot be honestly faced in English terms alone. This leads the author into a

*Daniel Jenkins *The British: Their Identity and Their Religion* (London: SCM, 1975)

John S. Dunne *The Way of All The Earth: An Encounter with Eastern Religions* (London: Sheldon, 1973)

survey of the 'Matter' of Britain, of Scotland, and of Wales, followed by a much lengthier study of 'The English and Their Churches', in the course of which he appeals for the recognition of a distinctively Scottish and a distinctively Welsh national identity in a way that deserves consideration not only by English Christians but by English Buddhists as well.

Committed English, Scottish, and Welsh Buddhists alike, however, will hardly agree with what he has to say about Eastern religion, very briefly discussed in the concluding paragraph of a section on 'Other religious groups in England'. Indeed, they may well find his attitude towards them no less patronizing than he finds the attitude of the English towards the Scots and the Welsh. One would have thought that Professor Jenkins would have known what it was like to be a member of a religious minority! 'It is fashionable at present,' he observes, 'among some self-conscious people to say that Western tradition is bankrupt and that the inherited values of England, those of her religion and patriotic loyalty and family life, must be repudiated. This carries with it a new interest (it can hardly be much more than that at present) in Eastern religion, notably some forms of Buddhism, and in the view of the world associated with it. One could not look to such an attitude for a renewal of the English vision, since part of its point would be to deny the validity of such a vision' (p. 122). What this English vision is the author does not tell us, though since he is at pains to distinguish England from Britain we must assume that it is not quite the same thing as the British ideal, which in a chapter on 'The Community of Britain' he finds to consist in a tension between the 'Cavalier' and 'Roundhead' elements in our tradition, as well as in the qualities of respect for privacy, modesty, fair play, and moderation — an ideal that plainly has its limitations, as he himself admits.

We must also assume, no doubt, that the vision is a Christian vision. But if this is the case, then surely the (absolute) validity of the English vision is denied not only by the self-conscious people who are 'interested' in Buddhism and other Eastern faiths but by hundreds of thousands, perhaps millions, of people in these islands who have not even heard of Buddhism! Professor Jenkins rebukes John Cowper Powys for invoking the ancient pre-Christian Brythonic God instead of 'the Christian God, who is the Father of us all' (p. 53). What he fails to realize is how many there are to whom the Christian God is as unreal and as remote as the Brythonic God is to him. However much we are all agreed that Britain is spiritually sick, and that a national renewal is possible only on the basis of a religious renewal, it by no means follows that the renewal has to be — or even can be — a Christian one. The fact is that the majority of people in Britain are no longer Christian. They do not believe in the Christian God. Indeed, in his concluding chapter, 'Jerusalem and Albion: The Christian Community', Professor Jenkins admits that 'the chief reason why the British churches are weak today is that they do not believe enough in the Christian God whom they profess to serve' (p. 18). Those who do not believe that religious renewal is possible on the basis of Christianity because they do not believe in Christianity are therefore faced with two alternatives. They must either give up all hope of any renewal or they must look for the vision that will bring it about *outside Christianity*. To Professor Jenkins, of course, the second alternative is unthinkable. For him, all the viable options are within the Christian faith. The reason for this shortsightedness is to be found partly in the fact that his original point of departure is communal life in modern Britain rather than the individual in modern Britain. It is in fact the main weakness of Professor Jenkins' book that his thesis assumes too much. Our national consciousness and our religious — i.e. Christian — heritage may indeed have been closely linked in the past, but before considering how the churches can help bring about a renewal of the communal life of Britain we must surely ask ourselves how acceptable Christianity itself still is to the individual Briton.

John S. Dunne is currently Professor of Religious Studies at Yale University, and has been hailed (by *Newsweek*) as 'the only forseeable successor to Paul Tillich'. As benefits one who has studied at Notre Dame University in America and at the Gregorian University in Rome, he has written a subtler and more scholarly book than Professor Jenkins and one that is seemingly more liberal. His thesis is that what seems to be occurring in our time is a 'passing over' from one culture to another, from one way of life to another, from one religion to another, and that this 'passing over' is followed by an equal and opposite process of 'coming back', coming back with new insight to one's own culture, one's own way of life, one's own religion. The holy man of our time is not a man who could found a new religion, but a figure like Gandhi, a man who passes over by sympathetic understanding from his own religion to other religions and comes back again with new insights to his own. According to Professor Dunne this passing over and coming back is the spiritual adventure of our time, and it is an odyssey that takes one not only through the wonderland of other religions back into the homeland of one's own religion, but also through the lives of prophets and divine incarnations back into one's own life. After beginning his odyssey by passing over into the life of Gandhi, and his renunciation of sexuality and violence, he therefore goes on to pass over into, and come back from, the lives of the Buddha, Krishna, Jesus, and Mohammed.

In all this there is much that the Western Buddhist,

whether American or British, will find acceptable. 'Passing over' is in fact something that isvery well understood in Buddhism, especially, perhaps, in Mahayana Buddhism. Indeed, Śāntideva's great teaching of *parātma-parivarta* or 'Transference of the Other and the Self' can well be regarded as the classic, and mostradical,statement of this process in all spiritual literature. Whether Professor Dunne himself really succeeds in passing over into the lives of prophets and divine incarnations is however doubtful. In the case of the Buddha he certainly does not succeed very well. Though seeing clearly that 'The remarkable thing about Gotama the Buddha was that he walked alone, without a friend, even without a God' (p. 29) he is still able to ignore the testimony of the Pali texts and say, 'Gotama did not deny the existence of God or the existence of the soul (although his refusal to talk about the soul has ordinarily been interpreted in this way); he simply refused to offer any teaching on them' (p. 30). We are therefore not surprised when, some pages later, he finds that 'In our effort to re-enact the life of Gotama we have found it necessary to try passing over to a standpoint of providence or universal care,' and triumphantly concludes, 'We might have suspected that God would figure somehow' (p.60). Indeed we might! For all his protestations, Professor Dunne does not really pass over from his own religion at all, but in fact carries his theistic assumptions with him in to non-theistic Buddhism. He even finds the Buddha's description of the middle way in terms of the Eightfold Path 'unhelpful', having apparently not 'passed over' into the Buddhist scriptures sufficiently to discover the meaning of rightview, right resolve, and the rest of its constituent factors. Despite some illuminating comments on the Four Sights, and on the Buddha's 'four confidences' one is therefore left with the overall impression that in reality there has been no passing over at all, not even in thought, and that Professor Dunne has been engaged in the performance of an elaborate exercise — not to say a skilful piece of play-acting, or even a conjuring trick — the purpose of which is to return the Western reader safely to his Christian base after a carefully conducted tour of world religions. That this is not just a construction arbitrarily imposed upon the book by the ill-natured non-Christian critic is borne out by what another Christian academic, Geoffrey Parrinder, writes in the introduction. 'It is often thought that acquaintance with other religions will weaken our own. One of the chief merits of Professor Dunne's book is his evidence that the opposite can happen. Far from faith being undermined, it can be enlarged and strengthened by wider studies and by looking at our own religion from other angles.' As a general principle few Western Buddhists would wish to dispute this. What they would strenuously deny was that, as all three Christian academics seem to assume, one's 'own' religion is necessarily the religion that one was born into. Such an assumption gives far too much importance to cultural factors. Neither Professor Jenkins nor Professor Dunne faces up to the fact that times have changed, and that an individual Westerner now may, in all seriousness, commit himself to a religion other than the one into which he was born, and which forms part of his national heritage. For this reason Professor Jenkins is unable to envisage a spiritual renewal for Britain except on the basis of Christianity. Similarly, Professor Dunne is unable to imagine anyone passing over from Christianity into another religion *and staying there*. Professor Jenkins indeed goes so far as to say, 'Those who know the love and power of the Father can be confident that, in due time, the prodigals will come to themselves and want to return' (p. 195). What both Christian academics fail to realize — what academics in general fail to realize — is that some of the prodigals, at least, have gone for good, and that whether in peremptory or in dulcet tones it is no longer any use trying to call them home.

Hedonism and the Spiritual Life*

This is one of those entertaining and instructive essays in cultural anthropology that, over the last two or three decades, we have learned to expect from the campuses of North America. In his preface the author tells us that the book aims at showing up the common base of 'the trimmings of transcendental meditation, the Hare Krishna gymnastics, the dilated smiles of Jesus freaks, and the now defunct hippydom of the sixties' through their common errors, and that 'as such it aims to be a perennial critique of mystical movements and of utopia in general' (p. 10). Agehananda Bharati is well equipped for the task. Born and brought up in Vienna, where he began studying Sanskrit and other Indian languages while still a boy, he served during World War II as an interpreter in Hitler's 'Free India' legion and then, after two years of Indology and philosophy, in 1949 he made his way to India. In India he stayed for seven years, during which time he became a Hindu monk, taught at universities, and upset orthodox Hindus with his 'cultural criticism'. He left India rather under a cloud as I remember from newspaper reports published at the time. After surfacing in Thailand and in Japan, he eventually reappeared in the New World, where from the late fifties onwards he has taught classes,

*Agehananda Bharati *The Light At The Center: Context and Pretext of Modern Mysticism* (Ross Erikson/Santa Barbara, 1976)

criticized, and copulated on the spacious campuses of North America. In 1961 he published *The Ochre Robe*, a provocative mélange of autobiography and cultural criticism. This was followed by *A Functional Analysis of Indian Thought and its Social Margins* (1964), which I have not seen, and *The Tantric Tradition* (1965), an important study mainly from Hindu Sanskrit sources.

According to the publishers *The Light at the Center*, his latest book, is an investigation of mysticism in the tradition of Butler, Underhill, and Zaehner. This it certainly is not. The author's approach is synchronistic rather than historical, and despite much preliminary flourishing of ethnoscientific and ethnosemantic tools — now *de rigeur* in the religious field it would seem — the work is on the whole belletristic rather than scholarly. *Time Magazine* goes so far as to say ' . . . Bharati unscrews the inscrutable with the precision tools of language, philosophy, and behavioural sciences'. He does not quite do that, but evidently it is what he sees himself as doing. Despite his efforts the inscrutable is *not* unscrewed, and though light is thrown on a variety of topics no generally acceptable definition of mysticism emerges. This is hardly surprising. 'Mysticism' is one those protean words that elude precise definition, and for this reason I personally prefer not to use it. Instead of arguing whether Agehananda Bharati's definition is correct, and whether mysticism is 'really' what he says it is, I shall therefore take his definition at its face value and try to see whether what he calls mysticism corresponds to anything with which we are familiar within the context of Buddhism.

As defined by him, mysticism is the *'intuition of numerical oneness with the cosmic absolute, with the universal matrix, or with any essence stipulated by the various theological and speculative systems of the world'* (p. 25, Author's italics). A mystic is a person who has experienced this numerical oneness, or seeks to experience it, and who, when questioned about his most important pursuit, consistently says '*I am a mystic*' in the *etic* sense rather than in an *emic* sense (i.e. in the generally accepted meaning of the term, not in the meaning which it has for a particular coterie). Agehananda Bharati himself is a mystic, as are the Buddha, Ramakrishna, Ramana Maharshi, Arthur Koestler, Timothy Leary, Alan Watts, Allen Ginsberg, and Aldous Huxley. All have had the zero-experience, as Bharati also terms the intuition of numerical oneness with the absolute, although in Huxley's case there appears to be some doubt about it. A mystic is also a person who, in seeking numerical unity with the absolute, does so by espousing psycho-experimental methods which are hedonic rather than non-hedonic. Among these methods are sexual and aesthetic experience and the use of psychedelic drugs. For Bharati the achievement of pleasure, euphoria, ecstasy, is central to the mystic quest, and with this we come to the real crux of his whole discussion of the subject matter of the book — whether called mysticism or any other name. As he sees it, mysticism is that form of religious life or religious experience in which the pleasure-principle reigns supreme. This is not to say that he denies that the zero-experience can be triggered off with the help of non-hedonic, ascetic psycho-experimental methods: it is simply that the possibility does not interest him, and he therefore does not concern himself with it. In his own words, 'Rejection of euphoria does not disqualify a person from the mystic title: but he falls into a somewhat marginal category' (p. 27). Yet despite its supremacy in its own sphere, the pleasure-principle affords us no access to the domain of the reality-principle. Bharati makes it quite clear that while mysticism is the intuition of numerical oneness with the absolute it does not follow from this that the absolute actually exists. The zero-experience does not confer ontological status on its own content. What really happens is that a thought chain occurs which is felt by the mystic as meaning that he has achieved oneness with the absolute (p. 11). From this it follows that the zero-experience does not entail a specific theology or ideology, or any specific type of action or inaction (p. 69). Similarly, the zero-experience does not change the mystic in any respect, though it may alter his self-image and, in this way, bring about a change in his environment by changing people's attitudes towards him. In particular, the zero-experience does not make the mystic a better man. The stinker remains a stinker. Indeed, as if rubbing it in, Bharati assures us that 'some of the best mystics were the greatest stinkers among men' (p. 91) and that 'mystics can be saints, they can be vicious tyrants, or anything else' (p. 124). He does, however, concede that the mystic arranges his deeds and thoughts in a hierarchy with the zero-experience at the top and the rest in a descending scale of importance below (p. 102) — a concession which has the effect of undermining his whole position. Bharati also believes that it is unimportant how the mystic comes by the experience (p. 112) — a view that separates means and end, that it is 'in one category perhaps with totally consumated erotic experiences, or with artistic and similar peak sensations' (p. 75), and that, if a person who has had the experience 'dislikes' it, he can 'of course' have it analysed — i.e. psychoanalysed — out of him (p. 143). The mystical experience is what it is. It is to be sought not because it is noble, but simply because it is a skill which confers delight, and because it 'inures the practitioner against the vicissitudes of life, against boredom and despair' (p. 78). This is an arid message, Agehananda Bharati admits, to 'those who have expected to find the ultimate panacea of the religious and the secular life in the mystical' (p. 75), but there's nothing he can do about it: the zero-experience is really all there is.

Arid though the message may be, there is nothing arid about the way in which the author delivers it. He delivers it, in fact, not only with refreshing candour but with panache. Not that his candour is likely to be appreciated in the quarters where it is most needed. Some of his harsher strictures may indeed be found deeply offensive by the 'sanctimonious little men who impress the gullible by their accent, their smell, their robe' (p. 174), i.e. by the urban, middle-class, English-educated swamis of the Hindu Renaissance who, in this book as in *The Ochre Robe*, are the favourite targets of Bharati's cultural criticism. To the extent that they have the wit to perceive that it applies to them too, it will also be found deeply offensive by the swami's opposite numbers in Buddhism, i.e. the globe-trotting bhikkhus of South-east Asia who flit from capital to capital purveying the corresponding brand of 'pietistic talk' (p. 35). Those who are genuinely interested in the 'Wisdom of the East', and who are tired, perhaps, of the pseudo-spiritual claptrap of the pompous gurus and the 'stink of occidental adulation' that surrounds them, will welcome Agehananda Bharati's straightforwardness. They will be glad to hear him denouncing the 'glib and quite dangerous guru mania' (p. 200), as well as the warning against the 'pathological eclecticism' that permeates the entire counter culture (p. 37) and the 'latent Hindu fascism which, fortunately for the world, has no power except in India' (p. 199). Swami Vivekananda and the Ramakrishna Mission come in for especially severe handling. Bharati is 'certain that Vivekananda has done more harm than good to the seekers of mystical knowledge' (p. 154). As for the Ramakrishna Mission, its dozen or so centres in Europe and America are well established and stagnant, and their clientele has not changed in twenty years. The swamis in charge as well as their flock are against experimentation of any sort; the 'patently mystical directive' of their official monism is watered down to a respectable Sunday sermon, and the swamis 'vie with each other in giving establishmentarian, ecclesiastic advice, very much like the most average protestant ministers in the cities until thirty years ago' (p. 34). Once again, Bharati's criticism applies beyond its immediate context: we have our Ramakrishna Missions in Buddhism too.

Among the things for which Bharati most strongly criticizes both the swamis of the Hindu Renaissance and their 'grassroots' Indian counterparts is what he regards as their 'puritanical' attitude towards pleasure. Puritanism is in fact his *bête noir*, and although the word does not appear as often in *The Light at the Center* as it does in *The Ochre Robe*, and is not listed in the index, the earlier anathemas are still clearly in force. Whether a term of such distinctly Anglo-American provenance as 'puritanism' can really be applied in this naïvely uncritical fashion to Indian religious life is more than doubtful, but we perhaps should not be over rigorous. By puritanism Bharati appears to mean any disposition to check the totally uninhibited enjoyment of the fullest possible (hetero-) sexual pleasure. As an example of modern Hindu puritanism he cites the attitude of scholars and others to the ananda-mimamsa or 'pleasure scale' of the *Taittiriya Upanishad*, which according to him they reject. Prof. J. L. Mehta, for instance, 'got furious' when he quoted it (p. 63). To the best of my recollection, far from rejecting the ananda-mimamsa, or 'beatific calculus' as some of them call it, modern Hindu scholars and swamis, — even the etiolated swamis of the Ramakrishna Mission, refer to it and expatiate on it *ad nauseum*. Indeed, I sometimes used to think that there was far too much bliss talk in Hindu religious circles. Bharati's discussion of the subject is not very clear. According to the ananda-mimamsa, a hundred measures of human bliss, i.e. the bliss experienced by a healthy well-educated young man in possession of the riches of the whole world, equal one measure of bliss on the scale of the human gandharvas; a hundred measures of bliss on the scale of the human gandharvas equal one measure of bliss on the scale of the divine gandharvas, and so on from the divine gandharvas to the ancestors and the ancestors to the gods by birth, etc., right up to a hundred measures of bliss on Prajapati's scale, which equal one measure of bliss on the scale of Brahman or 100,000,000,000,000,000,000,000 times the measure of human bliss (*Taittiriya Upanishad* I, 8). The general principle involved, that of the existence of a whole hierarchy of blissful experiences, from the grossest bodily to the most refined spiritual, is perfectly clear, and is accepted not only by all Hindus but also by all Buddhists and, probably, by all Christians as well. They also accept, as the practical corollary of this, that in order to pass from a lower to a higher degree of bliss it is necessary to detach oneself from, or grow out of, or transcend — the vocabularies vary — the lower degree of bliss. This is why the *Taittiriya Upanishad* as it enumerates each level of bliss, declares it to be equal not only to a hundred measures on the preceding scale but also to the measure of bliss 'of the man well versed in scripture *who is not smitten by desire,*' i.e. desire for the lower degree of bliss. As the *Dhammapada* says, 'If by renouncing limited bliss (*mattāsukha*) one can experience abundant bliss (*vipulaṁ sukhaṁ*), let the wise man renounce the limited bliss for the sake of abundant bliss' (*Dhammapada 290*). Herein hedonism and asceticism coincide. What Mehta and others who think like him reject is — so it appears — not the euphoric content of the mystical experience, as Bharati alleges, but the suggestion that a lower degree of bliss (e.g. sexual pleasure) is qua bliss identical with a higher degree of bliss (e.g. the bliss of

Brahman), so that there is no question of one being better or nobler than the other and no question, therefore, of detaching oneself from the lower degree of bliss in order to experience the higher degree, i.e. no question of asceticism. Bharati himself — in *The Ochre Robe* at least — takes the quantitative language of the *Taittiriya Upanishad* quite literally, denying that the quantitative changes of the pleasure scale ever change into qualitative ones. But in a sense he does not take it literally enough. So concerned is he to insist that sex and Brahman are equally bliss that he forgets that they are not equally blissful, thus depriving himself of all motivation for passing from the one to the other. But it is time for us to see whether what Bharati calls mysticism corresponds to anything with which we are familiar within the context of Buddhism — and time to look at his references to Buddhism.

One of the most basic distinctions in all Buddhism — basic to thought and spiritual practice alike — is the distinction between *śamathā* or 'calm' and *vipaśyanā* or 'insight', the one representing the entire range of dhyanic or superconscious experience, from the lowest discursive to the highest non-discursive, the other the direct, intuitive, wordless and conceptless confrontation with the ultimate reality of things. It does not take much reflection to see that the type of religious experience that Agehananda Bharati terms mystical coincides roughly with the lower levels of *śamathā* experience, which are hedonic and non-sensuous, plus the more intensely hedonic forms of sensuous experience. (On the higher levels of *śamathā* experience bliss is not present as a separate, distinguishable factor.) In terms of Buddhist psychology, the range of the mystical extends from the higher reaches of desire-world consciousness (*kāmāvacaracitta*) through all the levels of form-world consciousness (*rupāvacaracitta*) up to, and not including, the formless-world consciousness (*arūpāvacaracitta*), while in 'mythological' terms it extends from the heaven of the Four Great Kings and the heavens of the other gods of the desire-world up through the heavens of the Brahma gods, of the gods of limited, unlimited, and sonant light, of the gods of limited, unlimited, and wondrous beauty, and of the 'unconscious' gods as far as the gods of the 'pure abodes' (*suddhāvāsa*). In terms of the stages of the Path the mystical extends from the satisfaction and delight (*pramodya*) that arises in dependence on faith (*śraddhā*), through interest, enthusiasm, joy, rapture (*prīti*), and calmness, repose, tranquillity, serenity (*prasrabdhi*), up to bliss (*sukha*), and total psychical integration (*samādhi*) — these being, of course, the third to the seventh in the series of 'positive' *nidānas*. All these levels of *śamatha* — whether interpreted as states of consciousness, heavens, or stages of the Path — are characterized by euphoria, which gradually increases in intensity, though inasmuch as it is the concomitant of psychical integration the more intense it becomes the less it is possible to speak of it as a separate mental factor. *Śamatha-bhāvanā*, the cultivation or development (lit. 'making to become') of 'calm,' — one of the two most basic forms of Buddhist meditation, is therefore a cultivation or development of bliss. The meditative life is the blissful life. As the Buddha exclaims in the *Dhammapada* (verse 200): 'blissfully indeed we live, we that regard nothing as our own. Enjoyers of ecstasy shall we be, like the Gods of Sonant Light'. But although bliss — mysticism — is almost the whole of *śamatha* it is not the whole of the spiritual life — taking the spiritual to include the transcendental. It is not the whole of Buddhism. *Śamatha* has its limitations — limitations which make clearer still the extent to which mysticism in general and the zero-experience in particular, coincides with *śamatha*. They are: (1) *Śamatha* experiences are mundane (*laukika*), not transcendental (*lokuttara*, lit.

'world transcending'); they belong to the realm of the compounded or conditioned (*saṁskrita-dhātu*), not to the realm of the uncompounded or absolute (*asaṁskrita-dhātu*). In dependence on conditions they arise, and in the absence of those conditions cease. Pictorially speaking, they form part of the wheel of life, and revolve as it revolves — even though, towards the outermost edge of the wheel, each revolution may take — or seem to take — hundreds of aeons. All *śamatha* experiences being equally mundane, regardless of whether they are 'lower' or 'higher', Bharati is from the Buddhist point of view technically right in refusing to recognize any more than a quantitive difference between the successive degrees of mystical euphoria. (2) *Śamathā* experiences have no ontological content; that is to say, they do not in themselves constitute an experience of ultimate reality, and it is not possible for us to draw from them any conclusions about the nature of ultimate reality. The nature of ultimate reality is revealed only to insight (*vipaśyanā*) or 'wisdom' (*prajñā*). Although *śamatha* experiences, as such, are devoid of ontological content, they are important — even necessary — from the spiritual point of view in that they provide a basis for the development of *vipaśyanā* and thereby contribute, indirectly, to the attainment of enlightenment. *Śamathā* as transfigured by, and inseparably united with, the insight for whose development it provided the basis, is what is known as *Samādhi* in the more Mahayanistic usage of the term. (3) In the absence of *vipaśyanā*, *śamatha* experiences can — and often do — become the basis for the construction of various pseudo-ontologies or 'views' (*drishti*) which, although they may purport to reveal the nature of ultimate reality have, in fact, no genuine ontological content. Buddhism traditionally regards all forms of theism, for example, as originating in this way. (4) *Śamathā* experiences do not, of themselves, bring about any permanent or radical change in the person enjoying them. Temporary and superficial changes may, indeed, occur, but these are doomed to pass away as soon as the *samathā* state itself comes to an end. Like a stretched-out piece of elastic, the mind reverts to its original position as soon as the expanding agency is removed. Only insight into the nature of ultimate reality is able to bring about permanent and radical change, by exposing the baselessness of the assumption that there exists, as the subject of *samathā* or any other experiences, a separate, unchanging, independent ego identity. Yes, *samathā* does have its limitations, and these limitations do indeed make clear the extent to which *samathā* coincides with mysticism or zero-experience as defined by Bharati. Both are blissful, both are unable to confer ontological status on their own content, and both are powerless to bring about any change in the meditator/mystic. Whether *both* can be analysed away remains to be seen. Bharati, Koestler & Co. are indeed mystics — as are some, at least, of the swamis of the Hindu Renaissance. We need not, as Buddhists, dispute the fact. By one means or another — or by no means — they have indeed enjoyed what in Buddhism are known as *samathā* experiences — experiences which were euphoric, without ontological significance, and which left them exactly as they were. But beyond *samathā* there is *vipaśyanā*. Beyond euphoria there is ultimate reality. Beyond Bharati, Koestler & Co., — beyond the swamis, — there is the Buddha.

That Bharati brackets himself and his fellow modern mystics with the Buddha almost as a matter of course is due neither to simple effrontery nor to megalomania, but to the fact that he is unable to distinguish between *samathā* and *vipaśyanā*, 'calm' and 'insight'. Because he is unable to distinguish between calm and insight he has no means of telling a mystic from a spiritually enlightened being. He has, also, no means of access to the 'ontological dimension': no means of access to ultimate reality. (The mystic's intuition of numerical oneness is only a *feeling*.) Brahmin teachers like Vasistha, Patanjali, and Sriharsa, he tells us, taught that the sources of information about 'the ontological status of divinity, or reality, of the cosmos', is 'the infallible word of the Veda' (p.85), a view which he as a Hindu apparently accepts. More than once, however, he refers to the rishis, the 'seers' of the mantra, the Vedic word, as mystics, and to 'canonical passages' as being 'statements made by people who have had the zero-experience' (p. 77). If the rishis are mystics the Vedas cannot be sources of ontological information, i.e. information about ultimate reality. Or is the ontological status conferred on the content of the rishi's experience by some means extraneous to the experience itself? Bharati does not say. Buddhism does not, of course, accept the Vedas as sources of ontological information, i.e. it does not accept their 'infallability'. For Buddhism too the rishis are mystics. That is why the Buddha — or rather the Bodhisattva — left Alada Kalama and Rudraka Ramaputra: they could teach him *śamathā*, but not *vipaśyanā*; they could not show him the way of Supreme Enlightenment. Bharati's references to ontology are not, in fact, very clear, and seem to be based on metaphysical assumptions of the 'common sense' order. According to Buddhist teaching, in ultimate reality there is no distinction of subject and object, and *vipaśyanā* or insight 'intuits' or 'reflects' this non-distinction. For Buddhism, therefore, there is no question, in the ultimate sense, of an ontology as distinct from an epistemology: *vipaśyanā* does not reveal an object — even a transcendental object — as distinct from a subject, but it 'reveals' an ultimate reality which, when made the object of thought and speech, — when brought within the dualistic framework of the subject-object relation, — can be regarded only as object as opposed to subject. In the Mahayana this ultimate reality is known as Śūnyatā. 'Śūnyatā' is not an object but a pseudo-object. As a term in spiritual discourse — in spiritual communication — it 'points out' or 'indicates' not a real ontological object but an ultimate reality that transcends the duality of subject and object, ontology and epistemology. In the same way, Buddhist ontology is a pseudo-ontology, or rather, a symbolical ontology — in the mathematical rather than the Jungian sense. Just as 'Śūnyatā' does not indicate a real ontological object, even though the exigencies of language compel us to say of it that it *is* neither existent nor non-existent, so the conceptual constructions of Buddhist 'ontology' (a term I use only because Bharati uses it) do not purport to mediate a world of really existing metaphysical objects to a really existing epistemological subject but have, instead, the function of 'pointing out' a condition of ultimate reality in which the distinction of subject and object does not obtain and of providing, moreover, a practical support for the development of insight or wisdom (*prajñā*). Bharati does not, it seems, understand this. Though he correctly says that Nagarjuna, as a Buddhist, 'denied ontological status to any experience', i.e. to any mystical (=*śamathā*) experience, and that 'he did not feel that the zero-experience could add anything to the experiencing person's knowledge about the world' (pp. 82-83), this does not mean, as he seems to think it does, that for Nagarjuna there is no ultimate reality beyond the zero-experience. *As a Buddhist*, Nagarjuna affirmed the 'existence' of such an ultimate reality, which he termed Śūnyatā, and which was to be realized by wisdom, or rather by the perfection of wisdom (*prajñā-pāramitā*).

Though Buddhism plays only a very minor part in Bharati's book (Zen does not interest him — p. 185), it is apparent from his occasional references to it that his knowledge of it is neither wide nor deep. He shows no acquaintance with primary sources, on the importance of which he places great emphasis in the case of Yoga and Vedanta, and seems, in fact, to rely for much of his information on the Buddhist equivalent of the Hindu Renaissance type of pamphlet literature which he so heartily despises. In one place he gives us (p. 135), without references, a greatly expanded — not to say 'spiced up' — and entirely apocryphal version of the Buddha's well known reply to Ananda's question as to how monks are to comport themselves with regard to women (*Dīgha-Nikāya* II, 141). In another, he tells us that, 'every single one', of the Buddha's speeches, 'starts with *bhikkhave*, "ye begging monks"; he never addressed anyone who wanted to stay out' (p. 133). Such slovenliness in someone who makes such a parade of scholarship as Agehananda Bharati does is quite breath-taking. Even a quick look at the middle fifty discourses of the *Majjhima-Nikāya*, the 'Collection of Middle Length Discourses', for example, would have shown him, out of a total of fifty discourses, ten addressed to householders (*gahāpati*), ten to non-Buddhist wanderers (*paribbājaka*), ten mainly to or about royalty, ten to brahmins, and only ten to the bhikkhus or begging monks. In any case, did not the Buddha exhort his first sixty spiritually enlightened disciples to journey forth for the welfare and happiness of many people (*bahujana*) and proclaim the Dharma? (*Vinaya-Piṭaka* I, 21) There is no question of his message being addressed only to monks, even though these might have formed the largest and most important section of his community.

Bharati's most serious misunderstanding, however, is in connection with Buddhist meditation, about which he has some quite odd ideas. 'In the Pure Land School of Northern Buddhism', he says, 'the Buddha is the giver of grace to those who worship him faithfully, with very little attention to the highly individualistic, speculative, and affect-less meditations which go with the Theravada and with many Mahayana schools' (p. 123). What these 'speculative' meditations are we can only guess, while as for them being 'affect-less', this is surely almost a contradiction in terms. As we have already seen, *śamathā* involves elements of delight, rapture, ecstasy, and bliss: the meditative life is the blissful life. There is also the example of the four Brahma Viharas, one of the most popular meditations with the Theravada and the Mahayana schools alike. Surely Bharati does not seriously mean to describe the meditative development of friendliness (*maitrī*), compassion (*karunā*), sympathetic joy (*pramuditā*), and equanimity (*upekshā*), as being 'highly individualistic, speculative, and affect-less'. Some of the more extreme representatives of the modern so-called '*vipassanā* meditation' (not to be confused with the traditional *vipaśyanā-bhāvanā* common to practically all forms of Buddhism) do, of course, believe that it is possible to develop *sukkha-vipassanā* or 'dry insight', i.e. insight that has not been 'moistened' by the blissful experiences of the dhyana states, and of this some rumour may have reached Bharati, but in general meditation teachers do not see the development of 'dry insight' as a practicable possibility. The whole notion of *sukkha-vipassanā* would appear to rest on a confusion between two radically different things: (1) Actual insight into ultimate reality, and (2) recollection of the doctrinal categories of the Abhidhamma. What may be termed the standard or classic formulation of the Buddhist spiritual path, the Buddhist spiritual life, sees it as progressing from ethical observance through ever higher levels of psychical integration and euphoria to insight and wisdom and, from these, eventually to enlightenment. The experience of dhyanic bliss, though itself mundane, is the means of transition from the mundane to the transcendental. Hedonism — the higher hedonism that coincides with asceticism — is an integral part of spiritual life. Enlightenment itself, indeed, can be thought of not in exclusively noetic terms but, rather, as the inseparable unity of ineffable Bliss and transcendental Awareness.

Despite its title, *The Light at the Center* conveys no inkling of this unity. On the contrary, there runs through the book a psychical cleavage that affects not only the author's whole approach to his subject but also the style with which he writes, e.g. mysticism is 'a highly structured pursuit of experiential maximization' (p. 91). Bharati is not unaware of the cleavage. 'I have long maintained,' he says, 'that the mystic who happens to be a scholar must live and think in a manner which psychiatrists call schizophrenic' (p. 82). This is to understate the matter. Bharati's 'schizophrenia' does not consist just in his being a mystic who 'happens' also to be a scholar. After all, what makes one a mystic — apart, of course, from saying that one is a mystic — is the zero-experience, and this, as he makes quite clear, is of very rare occurrence. The schizophrenia consists in the fact that, in the absence of *vipaśyanā* — and in the absence of any form of asceticism — Bharati is left not with mysticism and scholarship but with sexual and aesthetic euphoria and scholarship. Indeed, he is left with rather less than that. The gap between sense and intellect, the emotions and reason, can be bridged with the help of the fine arts, and the enjoyment of natural beauty, all of which have a unifying effect on the psyche. With the exception of classical and baroque music (played as he drives to work and while copulating) Bharati seems to be no more interested in these things, however, than he is in Zen. At any rate, there is no mention anywhere in his book of poetry, or of the visual arts, or of nature, nor anything to show that he is so much as aware of their existence. In the absence of the fine arts, therefore, and the enjoyment of natural beauty, he is left not with sexual and aesthetic euphoria and scholarship, even, but simply with sex and scholarship, or sex and academic research. If Gerald Scarfe was ever to caricature Agehananda Bharati, it would probably be as a pair of outsized genital organs hanging from an enormously overdeveloped brain — an image that might do equally well for some of his counterparts in the field of Buddhist studies.

Bharati's greatest mistake, perhaps, has been to ignore the part played by asceticism in the religious life and in religious experience. He knows that there is such a thing as asceticism, of course, but he brushes it aside or tries to forget about it — or confuses it with puritanism. Occasionally, however, the truth will out. 'The professional mystics in India,' he has to admit, 'are almost all monastics — they have obtained ordination in orders which enjoin celibacy' (p. 171). That seems clear enough. Later on, however, he says, 'The fact that most methods now taught for supreme religious consummation are of the ascetic order, is a complex series of historical accidents which I cannot go into' (p. 209). What these accidents are it would be interesting to know. Perhaps Bharati will be able to particularize them in another book. Meanwhile, we have this book, which despite serious limitations does do a number of useful things. It provides us with a highly individual critique — not to say exposé - of the India-originated religious movements, insists on the dysfunctional nature of eclecticism, and stresses the need for the would-be mystic to follow a genuine tradition. Above all, perhaps, it reminds us that pleasure is not something to be feared, and that the hedonistic element is an essential part of the quest of seekers in the West. Even though we still have to remember that hedonism — ecstasy — mysticism — śamathā — is only part of the spiritual life, not the whole of it, for ex-Christian Hindus and ex-Christian Buddhists alike, the reminder is still, no doubt, a salutary one.

Patterns of Non-violence*

The development of ethical ideas is inseparable from the development of consciousness. Nature is unconscious. Even at the level of organic existence, life is, to begin with, sentient rather than conscious, and even when, with the emergence of animal life, sentience develops into consciousness, it is simple consciousness that develops, not the reflexive consciousness that is the distinctive characteristic of human beings. Since nature is unconscious it is either 'mechanical' or instinctual rather than intelligent, and in each of its forms operates without regard for — because without (real) awareness of — any of its other forms. Nature is therefore the 'Nature red in tooth and claw' of the poet and does not so much shriek against man's creed as remain blind to the possibility of any such achievement. As it is weight and mass that count on the level of inorganic existence, so it is size and strength that count on the level of organic life. Nature is governed by 'power', and man, to the extent that he remains simply a part of nature, i.e. to the extent that he has not developed reflexive consciousness, — to the extent that he is not truly human, — is governed by power too. It is only when, as a result of the development of reflexive consciousness, he begins to realize that others are capable of suffering just as

*Unto Tähtinen *Ahiṃsā: Non-violence in Indian Tradition* (London: Rider, 1976)

he is, and that they would not like done to them what he would not like done to him, that ethical ideas develop. Human life then comes to be governed, to a limited extent at least, not by power, i.e. violence in the form of force or fraud, but by an entirely different principle. It comes to be governed by love, not in the sentimental sense, but rather in the sense of the Confucian *shu*, 'reciprocity' or 'altruism', or the Godwinian 'benevolence'.

In Indian tradition this higher principle finds expression in the idea of *ahiṃsā* or non-violence, which although grammatically negative in form stands for an ethical ideal that is positive as well as negative in content. Non-violence is, in fact, a key concept of Indian ethics, and there are six comprehensive philosophies of non-violence in Indian thought. In *Ahiṃsā: Non-violence in Indian Tradition*, a work based on original Sanskrit, Pali, Prakrit, and Tamil sources, the Finnish Indologist Unto Tähtinen compares, for the first time, the different meanings of *ahiṃsā* in Buddhism and Jainism, in the Hindu Vedas, Dharmaśāstras, and Puranas, and in the thought of Mahatma Gandhi and his followers. We are thus given an extremely comprehensive and detailed study which in nine short chapters covers the definition, the roots, and the nature of *ahiṃsā* 1, 3, 4), the nature of *hiṃsā* or violence (2), the relation between *ahiṃsā* and other moral norms, *ahiṃsā* and war, *ahiṃsā* and crime, *ahiṃsā* and sub-human beings (5-8), and *ahiṃsā* in contemporary Indian life and thought (9).

One does not have to read very far in this study before becoming aware of the extent to which the idea of *ahiṃsā* or non-violence permeates the Indian religious consciousness, especially in the post-Vedic period, and the thoroughness with which Buddhism and Jainism, in particular, discuss the subject. In their concern for the practice of absolute non-violence, without the slightest taint of violence, the Jains, in the person of Amitagati, enumerate 432 types of *hiṃsā*, and there are other enumerations almost as elaborate. As Dr Tähtinen observes, however, such enumerations could be carried on *ad infinitum*: 'The basic distinction appears to be that of violence in thought, word, and deed, which, in addition, may be directly committed, commissioned, or consented to. These classifications are common to all schools of thought' (p. 16). Non-violence itself is no less thoroughly discussed. Here too there is a good deal of common ground. Though the word *ahiṃsā* is often popularly understood as 'non-killing', all the philosophical schools take it in the broader sense of 'non-injury', and most of them regard this as being mental and verbal as much as, or even more than, physical. Nevertheless there are two distinct traditions of non-violence in Indian thought, the Vedic or brahmanic, and the ascetic or sramanic. According to the latter, which comprises mainly Buddhism and Jainism, non-violence is a universal principle and should be practised towards all living beings without exception. 'The ascetic conception of *ahiṃsā*', says Dr Tähtinen, 'differs from the Vedic conception by not including any form of justified violence into the idea of *ahiṃsā*. Nor does it imply that any type of *hiṃsā* is morally good' (p. 8). 'Thus the ascetic *ahiṃsā* is extended to every living being without exception. This implies that injury to an enemy, harm done to a criminal, or to an attacking beast, are to be termed as violence. It is this ascetic concept of non-violence which is applied universally' (p. 53). According to the Vedic or brahmanic tradition, on the other hand, non-violence is not a universal principle and should be practised only towards non-violent beings. 'It is not applicable to enemies in war, to criminals, wicked people, offending beasts, and animals to be sacrificed or killed for one's livelihood' (p. 52). Killing such beings as these one commits no sin: such *hiṃsā* is in fact *ahiṃsā*. Indeed, as Krishna reminds Arjuna in the *Bhagavad-Gita*, by refusing to wage righteous war a kshatriya or member of the warrior caste incurs sin. War is an open door to heaven, or, as the *Varaha-Purana* says, 'Those braves who die for the *brāhmanas*, their milk cows and their state go to the city of Indra, or heaven' (p. 93).

Although ascetic non-violence is universal, i.e. to be extended to all living beings without exception, this does not mean that there will not be degrees in its application. On account of the very nature of his position the layman will not be able to practise non-violence to the same extent as the monk. Nonetheless both are practising one and the same principle, the universal principle of non-violence: there is not one principle for the monk and another for the layman. 'According to the ascetic branch of thought a layman's ethics are the morality prescribed for a monk, though in a much diluted form' (p. 12). Collating various Pali Buddhist texts the author therefore says, 'A definite distinction can be drawn between the non-violence of a monk and that of a householder. Household life is full of hindrances and it is difficult for a man who dwells at home to live the higher life in full. As free as the air, so is the life of him who has renounced all worldly things. A householder is bound to destroy other living beings, but a monk practising self-restraint protects living beings. A |lay| Buddhist should at any rate avoid the practice of tormenting others (*para-paritāpana*) and not earn his livelihood as a cattle-butcher, a pig-killer, fowler, deer-stalker, hunter, fisherman, thief, executioner, jailer, or through any other cruel occupation (*kukūrakammanta*)' (p. 29). According to Jaina sources, 'When one is engaged in complete abstention |from violence| one becomes a saint. He who is engaged in partial restraint (*ekadesha-virati*) is only a disciple (*upāsaka*)' (p. 61). In Vedic or brahmanic non-violence there are also degrees of application, as of the monk and the layman, but with a vitally important difference. If the general duty of *ahiṃsā*, which according to Manu is applicable to all the four castes, comes into conflict with caste-duties or specific duties, e.g. the warrior's duty to fight or the king's duty to inflict punishment, then the caste-duties have preference (p. 56). Above all, if it comes into conflict with the Vedic injunction to kill animals in sacrifice, then non-violence must give way to violence (p. 5). In the words of the Mimamsa principle as stated by Khandadeva: 'The specific rule of killing at sacrifices is stronger than the general rule of prohibiting killing' (p. 35). Animal sacrifices are, in fact, good for all, including the animals slaughtered (p.35). Indeed Samkara, the celebrated exponent of non-dualist (*advaita*) Vedanta, declares that such sacrifice 'purifies the heart of a truth-seeker and ultimately awakens the desire to know the highest truth (*brahman*)' (p. 22). According to another source, however, the killing of animals in sacrifice having been enjoined on man by the divinely authoritative Vedas, whatever merit or demerit may accrue from the performance of such sacrifices goes to God (p. 5).

Since for the ascetic schools non-violence was a universal principle they refused to agree that it must give way to caste duties or to the Vedic injunction to kill animals in sacrifice, and this led them to deny the authority of the Vedas. To them violence was violence, and any attempt to argue that killing is justified because enjoined by the infallible Vedas only made matters worse by adding to the sin of violence the no less serious sin of ignorance (*āvidyā*). They therefore attacked the authority of the Vedas vigorously. In fact, it is difficult to say whether the opposition of the ascetic schools to the slaughter of animals in sacrifice, and with it their rejection of the Vedas, was the cause or the effect of their belief in non-violence. As Unto Tähtinen puts it, 'The vehement opposition against killing at sacrifices was a good cause for the protagonists of *ahiṃsā*. The extreme care of animal life might have originated in view of the fact that *ahiṃsā* flourished as a reaction against the ritual slaughter of animals. Non-violence did not come to be generally recognized so much as a reaction against injury done to men (e.g. in war) rather than as a profound opposition to the institutionalized killing of animals. The heterodox schools lived and prospered on this reaction, and their position was buttressed by the simultaneous denial of the authority of the Vedas' (pp. 37-38). This reaction against killing animals was, like the reaction against meat-eating, more the work of Jainism than Buddhism, possibly because Jainism was older than Buddhism and because at the time of Parshva (8th century BCE) animal sacrifice was more widespread than in the Buddha's day. 'The Buddha emphatically and persistently fought against such social maladies as robbery, strife, fear of violence, and use of intoxicants. He paid more attention to these social evils than the Jains, who were more concerned about the slaughter of animals at sacrifice. This seems to have provided a good reason for the spread of Buddha's doctrine' (p. 48). But if the Buddha's opposition to animal sacrifice and meat-eating was less emphatic than that of the Jainas He was more concerned than they were about violence against oneself. They approved of self-mortification, whereas He regarded it as an extreme to be avoided. They maintained 'that man, under specific conditions, will be morally advised to kill himself' (p.26), whereas He did not maintain any such thing. 'According to Pali Buddhism,' says Dr Tähtinen, 'suicide is not to be approved' (p. 24). There is, however, the curious case of the monk Godhika, whose suicide — committed after he had gained 'temporary release' for the seventh time — was apparently not disapproved of by the Buddha (*Saṃyutta-Nikāya* I, 123). Moreover, in the *Sadharma-puṇḍarīka Sūtra, XXII,* also not mentioned by Dr

Tähtinen, the Bodhisattva Sarvasattvapriyadarśana burns his own body with the object of worshipping the Buddha and His teaching of the Dharma and this heroic act is applauded by innumerable Buddhas

Important as the idea of non-violence undoubtedly is, it is not the only form in which the principle of love — the higher principle that emerges when man ceases to be governed solely by the principle of power — finds expression in Indian tradition. This is particularly so in the case of Buddhism. Despite the fact that *ahiṃsā* is listed in the Abhidharma as one of the positive mental events, i.e. one of the dharmas present in all wholesome/skilful mental states, the actual term *ahiṃsā* or non-violence does not occur nearly so frequently in Buddhism as it does in Jainism, for example. Jainism regards even sexual abstinence and truthfulness as forms of non-violence, and in fact tends to interpret the whole religious life in terms of the practice of this one all-important virtue. Buddhism does not do this. Buddhism speaks not only of non-violence but also, no less frequently, of non-cruelty (*avihiṃsā*), while the first of its five (or ten) precepts takes the form of abstention from injury to living beings (*pānātipātā veramaṇī*) — not abstention from killing, as Unto Tähtinen seems to think (p.79)*. So far as Buddhism in fact is concerned, the higher principle of love finds its richest and most characteristic expression in the twin concepts of *mettā* or universal friendliness and *karuṇā* or universal compassion. In the words of Dr Tähtinen's summary 'In Jainism the whole ethic revolves around the concept of *ahiṃsā*, in Buddhism other terms are stressed. *Mettā* or universal friendliness is of central ethical importance in Pali Buddhism, whereas *karuṇā* acquires this position in Sanskrit Buddhism. We may say that both *mettā* and *karuṇā*

---

*But see *The Ten Pillars of Buddhism* p.48

imply *ahiṃsā'* (p. 79). Both *mettā* and *karuṇā* also imply, needless to say — as does the concept of *ahiṃsā* itself — that vivid awareness of the existence of other people, that keen sensitivity to their joys and sorrows, which arises from the development of reflexive consciousness and in which true humanity consists. *Mettā* and *karuṇā* find their highest expression in the life of the Bodhisattva. 'A *Bodhisattva* will, by his every bodily, verbal, and mental action, regard only his fellow creatures. The mighty compassion (*mahā-karuṇā*) has as its object the good of all living beings. The mighty compassion is the antidote to *hiṃsā*. The *Bodhisattva* helps all living beings to enter the city of *nirvāṇa*. This can be facilitated by the transference of merit in the sense of eternal happiness radiated by all the *buddhas*. Compassion is extended to the limits of speculation. Non-violence assimilates and submerges into the notion of compassion' (p. 78). Since the principle of love finds its most characteristic expression in friendliness and compassion we are not surprised that 'For the Buddha non-violence seems to have been mainly mental' (p.68) and that He 'wished to cut violence at its root rather than tackle its manifestations' (p. 69). Such an emphasis is fully in accordance with the general nature of Buddhism which, in the words of one of the contemporary interpreters cited by Dr Tähtinen, is 'essentially a mind-culture'.

In modern times the concept of non-violence is for many people associated with the name Mahatma Gandhi. Within the context of contemporary Indian thought Gandhi represents the ascetic tradition of non-violence, just as Aurobindo represents the Vedic tradition of non-violence which, says Dr Tähtinen, 'has survived to the present day, and may appeal even now to the large majority of Indians and particularly politicians' (p. 116). Gandhi, who sometimes called himself 'a practical idealist', understands non-violence as essentially mental behaviour and regards it as involving dissociation of oneself from evil activities such as economic exploitation (p. 119). For him non-violence is a common duty, not a specific one. As Dr Tähtinen says, 'Gandhi's idea of *ahiṃsā* was not based on the Vedic conception of *ahiṃsā*. He ruled out all exceptions in the application of *ahiṃsā*. He derived his *ahiṃsā* from the ascetic sources, and it was this ascetic or *śramaṇic* concept which he applied, for the first time, to politics and economics' (p. 121). More specifically, 'Gandhi pleaded to adopt non-violence in the practical life of social groups and nations. He tried to apply non-violence in every walk of life, domestic, institutional, economic, and political. He knew of no case in which non-violence would not have provided a good guiding principle of action' (p. 123). This more extended application of the concept of non-violence — of the principle of love — is of great significance today. As Dr Tähtinen reminds us in the preface to his study, the need for non-violence has become more pressing than ever before because of its manifold applications. Non-violence can be applied to the settling of colonial, racial, and other social problems, to the need for making a choice between world peace and total destruction, to the need for the control of pollution created by industrial processes and products, and to the conservation of natural resources and the non-exploitation of subhuman life. Before we can apply the principle of non-violence, however, we must understand it, and how better shall we be able to understand it than by thoroughly acquainting ourselves with the six comprehensive philosophies of non-violence that have appeared in the history of Indian thought, particularly with those connected with the ascetic schools? It is this which Unto Tähtinen's systematically organized and richly informative study enables us to do.

The Twain Shall Meet*

Unbelievable as it may seem, this is the first study of Yoga
and Indian philosophy to be published in the English
language. We have, to be sure, any amount of popular
books on Yoga, and quite a lot of learned tomes on Indian
philosophy; but never before, I think, have the two topics
been brought together and dealt with in comparative
fashion within the compass of a single volume. The reason
for this is not far to seek. In England, at least, Yoga and
Indian philosophy tend to be the preoccupation of two
different sorts of people, even of two different circles, one
of them very much larger than the other. When one thinks
of Yoga the picture that springs to mind is of the
overweight British matron in breathless pursuit of health
and beauty, whereas when one thinks of Indian
philosophy the picture that presents itself is of a wizened
academic poring over dusty oriental manuscripts in a
remote corner of one of the less prestigious departments of
one of our older seats of learning. Rarely, if ever, do the two
circles overlap. The British matron pursues health and
beauty with little thought of philosophy, Indian or
otherwise; the academic pores over his manuscripts
without ever suspecting that they might have some
bearing on the conduct of his own life. At last, however,

---

*Karel Werner *Yoga and Indian Philosophy* (Delhi, Varanasi, Patna:
Montilal Barnarsidass, 1977)

Yoga and Indian philosophy come together in the person of an Indologist who is at the same time a teacher of Yoga — or of a teacher of Yoga who is at the same time an Indologist. His conception of Yoga goes as far beyond that of the British matron as his conception of philosophy goes beyond that of the academic. The result is not only an increase of breadth but also an increase of depth. Yoga is not just a series of physical exercises but 'a consciously adopted system of training or pattern of behaviour aiming at enlarging or deepening man's direct experience of reality rather than his ability to describe or explain it' (p. xi). Similarly, philosophy is neither the history of philosophical opinions nor linguistic analysis but 'a constant endeavour of the human mind to describe and rationally explain experienced reality in clearly defined concepts and create an overall and systematic as well as intuitively penetrative picture of the world including man which satisfies man's intellectual curiosity or urge for formulated knowledge' (p. xi).

Born in Czechoslovakia, Karel Werner studied Western philosophy and Indology, and after obtaining his Ph.D. in 1949 became a lecturer in Sanskrit and Indian civilization in Olomouc University. In 1968 he emigrated to England, where since 1969 he has been the Spalding Lecturer in Indian Philosophy and Religion in the University of Durham. In addition to his academic work he teaches Yoga and has also published articles on Yoga and Buddhism in English, German, and Czech. *Yoga and Indian Philosophy* is his first book in English, and represents the fruit of more than three decades of study and personal involvement. The work consists of seven chapters. After a short introduction, in the course of which Yoga and philosophy are defined in the terms already quoted, the author opens with a widely ranging chapter on 'The Existential Situation of Man' in which stress is placed on the fact that, 'unlike in

Europe, philosophy in India has always been concerned
with the individual, his existential situation, his destiny
and salvation, i.e. with the final solution of the riddle of
man's existence' (p. 14). There then follow three chapters
on Indian philosophy and three on Yoga. In the first group
of chapters Dr Werner looks at the nature of the world, as
the stage on which the drama of man's search for absolute
freedom takes place, and gives us a survey of Indian
cosmology. He then explores the essence and destiny of
man, and reviews the various Indian conceptions of
salvation. Each chapter follows the same general pattern.
The Vedic and Upanishadic contribution to our
understanding of the world, man, and salvation having
been considered, we are given an account of the more
systematic teachings of the Sankhya, the Advaita Vedanta,
and Buddhism, both Theravada and Mahayana, on each of
these three topics. Reference is also made to the
Vishishtadvaita and Dvaita schools of Vedanta and to
Jainism, as well as to the philosophy of Aurobindo Ghosh,
which according to the author is deeply influenced by
Mahayana Buddhism. In the second group of chapters Dr
Werner deals with the origin and purpose of Yoga, as well
as with its relation to philosophy, with the schools of Yoga,
and with Yoga in the modern world. The second of these
chapters, on 'Schools of Yoga', contains sections on the
Yoga of Early Buddhism and the Yoga of Patanjali, the first
of these being a short but careful study of the Buddha's
Noble Eightfold Path. Probably the most important
chapters of the book and, with the possible exception of
the last one, those of the greatest general interest, are
chapters 1 and 5, on 'The Existential Situation of Man as
Reflected in European and Indian Thought' and 'Yoga, its
Origin, Purpose, and Relation to Philosophy', and these
will therefore be considered at slightly greater length.

Western philosophy begins with the cosmological

speculations of the Milesian school, and it is here —
according to Dr Werner — that we find the start of
extraverted investigation of the world and, therefore, of
that objective approach to reality, including man, that is so
characteristic of European thought. Strengthened by the
work of Plato and Aristotle, this 'objectivist' tendency
eventually led to the birth of science and its domination
over our lives and thought. Until quite recently Western
philosophy did not really concern itself with the existential
situation of the individual. Even though objective values
exist only when experienced by individual subjects, in the
quest for objectivity of values — for universally valid
general ideas — the experiencing individual was finally lost
sight of and, despite his rediscovery by the modern
existentialists, 'is still missing in the structure of our
scientifically oriented, objectivist civilization' (p. 2). In
India the situation is very different. For Indian philosophy
the important and central problem of investigation has
always been 'the nature of man and the means of
transcending his present limited situation' (p. 14). Apart
from not going to the extreme of totally objectifying reality
and divorcing it from intelligent consciousness, Indian
philosophy has always enjoyed a 'dialectical' relation to
religion, neither becoming subservient to religious dogma,
nor having the results of its investigations ignored by
religious thought. Above all, it has been kept in touch with
actual human experience through its relation with Yoga,
which 'has always been used in India on the one hand as
a means of confirming or testing the results of
philosophical investigation and speculation on
transcendence and on the other as a source of inspiration
and a stimulus for philosophical thinking' (p.15). From all
this, as well as on account of its 'phenomenological'
method and its humanism, it is obvious that Indian
philosophy has much in common with modern

existentialism. Like existentialism, it is concerned with despair or dread, with death, and with freedom. For Indian philosophy, however, freedom is no mere theoretical concept or philosophical problem. Freedom is an experience. It consists in one's actually rising above the limitations of the existential situation, i.e. in the experience of 'transcendence', and 'the only way to the achievement of the experience of transcendence is individual Yoga practice of some kind' (p.21). While recognizing that Yoga in the broad sense of the term is not confined to India (p.96), Dr Werner clearly believes that (Indian) Yoga has a part to play in the West. There is, for instance, 'the possibility of resorting to Yoga methods, or of deriving help from them when the philosophical quest has reached its utmost limit in conceptual analysis' (p. 98). At the same time, he sounds a note of warning. Owing to the separation of the two circles already mentioned, 'the popularization' of Yoga and its practice in the West is in the hands either of Eastern gurus with little or no understanding of the Western psyche and tradition or of Western amateurs with varying degrees of competence' (p. 99). Experimental research into Yoga is therefore necessary.

Though by no means a big book, *Yoga and Indian Philosophy* covers quite a lot of ground, and inevitably there are a number of topics which one wishes the author could have discussed more fully. Querying the applicability of Western evolutionary thinking to the history of Yoga, for instance, Dr Werner rightly points out that at a later stage of its history a religious tradition cannot ever be regarded as spiritually higher than it was at the beginning. The point would have been made clearer, perhaps, if he explained that, in this kind of context, evolution is a term which strictly speaking applies to the *individual* rather than to the religious tradition to which the individual is regarded as belonging. This would have involved defining the 'individual', as well as distinguishing him from the 'group' and the group from the 'spiritual community'. There are also topics in connection with which the Buddhist might find himself disagreeing with the author. Is the state of deep sleep really one of 'unification with the essence' (p. 54) or with 'the Universal Self' (p. 75) as Dr Werner, following the Upanishadic teaching, seems to think? Was it in fact the 'storehouse consciousness' (*ālaya vijñāna*) which was 'newly recognized' by C. G. Jung and by him called the 'collective unconscious'? (p. 50). Is traditional Buddhism really just 'silent' on the problem of what is the essence of man, and is the five khandha analysis of the Pali Canon 'purely an analysis of the empirical constituents of the human personality as accessible to his present experience'? (p. 61). My own difference with Dr Werner relates to his implied disparagement of poetry. Speaking of the Rig Veda, which he describes as an extensive collection of hymns comprising 'the reactions of the Indian mind to its encounters with experienced reality, both external and internal', he objects to the view of Western scholars like Macdonell that the Vedas are 'imaginative creations of poets' (p. 23). But is that view really so very far from the truth? According to Shelley a poem is 'the very image of life expressed in its eternal truth', poetry 'the record of the best and happiest moments of the happiest and best minds', and poets themselves 'the hierophants of an unapprehended inspiration'. If this indeed be so, then surely there could be no greater praise for the Vedas than to say of them that they were the imaginative creations of poets — especially when one considers what the word imagination meant not only to Shelley but also to Blake and Coleridge. After all, poetry is much more than versified fancies. Apart from whatever might be said on such topics such as these, however, there is little in Dr Werner's book to which either scholar or yogi could reasonably object. Mature and balanced in its approach, this pioneering exploration of an important field is clearly the product not only of the study of Indian philosophy but also of the practice of Yoga, and as such merits our respectful attention.

Religio-Nationalism in Sri Lanka*

When I met Walpola Rahula in 1945, in Ceylon (now Sri
Lanka), he was probably the best known — certainly the
most notorious — monk in the whole island. His thesis
that the Buddhist monk had the right to take an active part
in politics had split the entire Sangha into two factions, one
enthusiastically supporting, the other violently con-
demning, the stand he had taken. It was not until some
years later, however, when I was myself a monk, that I
really came to know anything about him. Sinhalese
bhikkhus whom I met in Calcutta in the 'fifties, on my
periodic visits to the Maha Bodhi Society's headquarters,
gave me a vivid account of the disturbing effect he had had
on the socio-religious life of Buddhist Ceylon. (By that time
he was living in virtual exile in Paris.) One of them, with
whom I was on particularly friendly terms, took the
trouble of giving me a general idea of the contents of
Rahula's famous book *Bhiksuvage Urumaya* or *The Heritage of
the Bhikkhu*, published in 1946. There matters rested for a
number of years. I met Walpola Rahula for the second time
in 1965 or '66, when he was on a visit to London, and in
the course of a conversation we had at the Ceylon Vihara it
became evident that despite a scholarly preoccupation
with Mahayana thought his ideas were as 'radical' as ever.

---

*Walpola Rahula, *The Heritage of the Bhikkhu* (New York: Grove Press,
1974)

Now, twenty-nine years after the publication of the original Sinhalese edition, comes an English translation of *Bhiksuvage Urumaya*, so that we are at last able to see for ourselves what the fuss was all about. To Western Buddhists the whole subject is, indeed, of special interest, inasmuch as the author has recently aired his views on 'The Future of the Sangha in the West' in two articles in *The Middle Way* (June and August, 1974). I shall therefore go through the whole book chapter by chapter, commenting on anything that seems deserving of special notice. In this way we shall be able to see what sort of heritage we in the West may expect to take over from the Sangha in the East — or at least from a section of the Sangha in Ceylon.

1. Buddhism and Social Service

On the whole this chapter draws attention to an aspect of Buddhism which is often overlooked, i.e. its concern for the material as well as for the spiritual well-being of man, and the author rightly draws attention to passages in the Pali canonical texts which represent the Buddha as advising people on their economic, social, and political affairs. Unfortunately, the chapter opens with the sentence 'Buddhism is based on service to others'. Such ambiguity as this can spring only from extreme confusion of thought, and we are therefore not surprised when, after referring to the Buddha's renunciation of Nirvana in his previous life as Sumedha the hermit, the author goes on to conclude the first paragraph of this chapter with the statement 'A true Buddhist should have the strength to sacrifice his own *nirvāṇa* for the sake of others' — it being assumed, apparently, that to such a true Buddhist Nirvana is as 'accessible' as it was to Sumedha. With the help of a truncated reference to the Buddha's well known exhortation to His first sixty *enlightened* disciples to wander from village to village preaching to people for their good and well-being (nothing is said about Him exhorting them to proclaim the Dharma, and to make clear the perfectly pure *brahmacarya* or holy life), as well as by means of the plethora of references to the Buddha's advice on purely secular subjects already referred to, the impression is created that 'a true Buddhist' is concerned with the promotion exclusively of the material well-being of humanity. In other words, having in effect dismissed Nirvana as a sort of anti-social selfishness, the Bodhisattva ideal is equated with the secular concept of social service. Could the degradation of a sublime spiritual ideal be carried further than this? Despite his extensive scholarship, the author seems totally unaware of the true significance either of the 'transcendental' state of Nirvana, the goal of the Theravada, or of the transcendental 'career' of the Bodhisattva, the ideal of the Mahayana schools.

Besides degrading the Dharma, Walpola Rahula denigrates the people to whom it was preached by the Buddha and His disciples as they travelled from place to place. 'Generally' he says, 'the villagers were poor, illiterate, not very clean, and not healthy.' What evidence there is for the greater part of the population of Northern India being poor (by what standard?), dirty, and unhealthy in the Buddha's time we are not told. Even quite a cursory reading of the Sutta and Vinaya Piṭakas conveys quite a contrary impression. Indeed, if the villagers had not been prosperous, in the sense of having sufficient food, clothing, and shelter, how would they have been able to support so large a number of monks, both Buddhist and non-Buddhist? As for their being illiterate, *of course they were.* With the possible exception of a few traders, who may have used writing for purposes of business correspondence, everybody in that society was 'illiterate' — including the Buddha and His disciples. Religion and culture were transmitted exclusively by oral means. To be illiterate did not imply any lack of education or culture — or even of Enlightenment. One cannot help thinking that Walpola Rahula has fallen victim to what a distinguished fellow-countryman of his called 'the bugbear of literacy'.

2. The Evolution of the Life of the Bhikkhu

Quite a few Buddhists, even in the West, seem to be under the impression that the Buddha drew up, once and for all, a code of discipline for His monks to which the 'orthodox' among them have adhered ever since. The author shows that this was not so, and that even during the lifetime of the Buddha 'the Rules of Discipline were introduced and changed and modified in accordance with changing economic and social conditions to suit times and places' (p. 11). He therefore rightly concludes that 'The Vinaya (the Code of Disciplinary Rules for the *Sangha*) is not an absolute truth; it is only a convention agreed upon for the orderly and smooth life of a social organization. As it should be conducted according to the social and economic changes to suit the place and the time, the Buddha laid down appropriate rules and also changed and modified them' (pp. 11-12). One would have thought, however, that if the Vinaya could be modified according to changed social and economic conditions, it could with even greater reason be modified in accordance with changed psychological and spiritual needs, but on this aspect of the subject the author has — perhaps characteristically — nothing whatever to say. His concern seems to be exclusively with the social and the economic. There is also a certain amount of semantic confusion in connection with the word 'democracy'. Democracy means a form of government in which the 'governed' govern themselves, whether directly or through their elected representatives. It is therefore inapposite to say that 'the Buddha's system of controlling *bhikkhus* was purely democratic' (p. 11). If He really 'controlled' them surely the system was not democratic, and if it had really been democratic, the bhikkhus would have *elected* Him as their 'undisputed master' — which is surely unthinkable. The dilemma illustrates the confusion which is created when popular concepts are used without too close attention to their meaning.

3. The Councils

These are the councils of Rajagaha, Vaisali, and Pataliputra, and the author's very brief summary follows the traditional Theravadin accounts. He brings them in, apparently, simply in order to make the point that the differences of opinion about the Rules of Discipline which had sprung up among the bhikkhus by the time of the second council, were all due to the fact that 'A hundred years after the death of the Buddha the economic and social structure as well as the outlook of the people must have undergone changes' (p. 13). Once again we hear nothing of any spiritual changes. However, the author agrees with Dr B. M. Barua, who in turn agrees with Dr Nalinaksha Dutt, that the rise of schools and sects within the Sangha during this period was a sign of health rather than of decay.

4. Introduction of Buddhism to Ceylon: The National Religion of the Sinhala People

According to Sinhalese tradition, Buddhism was introduced into Ceylon in the 3rd century BCE by the Arahant Mahinda, son of the Emperor Asoka. In reply to a query by the king of Ceylon, Mahinda is said to have declared that Buddhism could not be considered to have taken firm root in Ceylon unless and until a Ceylonese, born in Ceylon and of Ceylonese parents, ordained in Ceylon, learned and recited the Vinaya in Ceylon. In other words, Buddhism would not be established in Ceylon unless the Sangha there was completely autonomous, i.e. not dependent on the parent body in India — an attitude fully in accordance with the spirit of Buddhism. However, Walpola Rahula takes Mahinda's statement to mean much more than that. 'Mahinda's desire' he says, 'was to make Buddhism the national religion of the Sinhalese people. And so it happened . . . Buddhism became the state religion' (p. 17). For 2,200 years legal possession of the throne was the right only of Buddhists. In the 10th century a king declared that only Bodhisattvas should become kings of Ceylon! (Presumably those who became kings *were* Bodhisattvas.) In the 13th century the *Pujavaliya* declares that the Island of Lanka (Ceylon) belongs to the Buddha Himself. Religio-nationalism seems to have run wild. As if that was not bad enough, however, we are told that 'Historical evidence clearly shows that Buddhism existed as an institution of the Sinhalese monarchy' (p.18). In other words, Buddhism has been subordinated to the state. By the time we come to the end of the chapter, therefore, we are not surprised to find the author concluding 'Thus, because of the unity of the religion, nation, and state, *bhikkhus* began to participate in many ways in public affairs and in the freedom and protection of the nation' (p. 19). What this 'participation' involved we shall see in the next chapter.

5. Religio-Nationalism and the National Culture

'From the time of King Dutugamunu . . . religious and national fervour of both the laity and the *Sangha* began to grow intensely' (p. 20). The Sinhalese from the south, we are told, mounted a 'crusade' to liberate the nation and the religion from the foreign yoke (the capital had been occupied by a South Indian king), and Dutugamunu, 'the greatest of national heroes', after proclaiming that he was warring not for the pleasures of kingship but for the re-establishment of Buddhism, marched at the head of his advancing army carrying a spear *with a sacred relic of the Buddha enshrined in it*. Western Buddhists will no doubt wonder where they have heard all this before. But the story is not yet finished. 'In this decisive battle for the liberation of Buddhism and the Sinhalese,' Walpola Rahula relates, 'the *bhikkhus*, headed by their great Elders, did not remain in their cells' (p. 20). One bhikkhu, 'who was about to become an *arahant*,' disrobed and joined the army, a large number of the others accompanied the army into battle, and 'blessed and inspired by the presence of *bhikkhus*, the warriors fought with great courage and determination' (p. 21). In these circumstances we are not surprised to learn that 'From this time the patriotism and the religion of the Sinhalese became inseparably linked. The religio-patriotism at that time assumed such overpowering proportions that both *bhikkhus* and laymen considered that even killing people in order to liberate the religion and the country was not a heinous crime' (p. 21). Indeed when the victorious king one day became remorseful when he thought of the destruction of thousands of beings in battle, eight arahant bhikkhus, i.e. monks who had attained Nirvana, came to the king and assured him that he had committed no sin. Non-Buddhists, they declared, were no better than beasts! Once again, we cannot help wondering where we have heard all this before.

At this point, feeling perhaps that he has been rather carried away by his enthusiasm for religio-nationalism, Walpola Rahula seems to check himself. He has the grace to admit that the statement of the eight arahants, as recorded by the *Mahāvaṁsa* or Great Chronicle of Ceylon, is diametrically opposed to the teaching of the Buddha. Yet he is clearly unwilling to condemn it outright. 'It is difficult for us today either to affirm or to deny whether the *arahants* who lived in the 2nd century BCE did ever make such a statement' (p. 22). (Apparently they *could* have made it, then.) However, being concerned with precedents rather than principles, he does not allow the problem to bother him for very long. By the 5th century CE, when the *Mahāvaṁsa* was written, monks and laity alike had clearly recognized that working for the freedom and uplift of the religion and country was so important and noble that arahants themselves, they believed, had accepted the idea that the destruction of human beings for this purpose was not a very grave crime — and this is all the author really wants to know. 'It is evident', he says, 'that the *bhikkhus* of that time considered it their sacred duty to engage themselves in the service of their country as much as in the service of their religion' (p. 22). He then gives examples illustrating the national and cultural activities in which the bhikkhus engaged. Some of the activities are innocent enough. In the reign of King Dutugamunu we find arahants functioning as architects and bhikkhus rendering manual labour by supplying the masons with bricks and mortar. Later on, however, the monks play a leading part in politics and even decide who should occupy the throne. Walpola Rahula is therefore able to conclude, very much to his own satisfaction, that 'from the earliest period of Ceylon history to the recent past, it is abundantly clear that in addition to participating in numerous other responsibilities, the *bhikkhus* played a leading role even in the highly responsible political function of selecting a suitable king to rule the country' (p. 23).

6. Fundamental Innovations

The most important of these innovations was the writing down of the *Tipiṭaka*. Hitherto, of course, it had been preserved exclusively by oral means, but in the last century BCE — in the reign of King Valagamba (Vattagamani-

Abhaya), an invasion from South India, internal dissensions, and above all, the most disastrous famine in Ceylon history, between them brought about such unsettled conditions in the country that the elder monks, fearful for the future of the religion, decided to commit the Buddha's Teaching to writing. This was a courageous and far-sighted decision, and we cannot be sufficiently grateful to the ancient worthies who, at such a time, preserved the 'Pali' recension of the sacred tradition not only for the Buddhists of Ceylon but for the world. Unfortunately, however, besides committing the *Tipiṭaka* to writing they resolved that doctrinal study was more important than the practice of ethics and meditation. As Walpola Rahula points out, this was directly contrary to the original teaching of the Buddha, according to which the practice of virtues and the realization of Nirvana were more important than the mere study of the Dharma. Not that this was not realized at the time. There was a lengthy debate between the *Paṃsukūlika* or ascetic 'rag-robed' *bhikkhus* and the *dhammakathika* or 'Dharma expounding' *bhikkhus*, but in the end the latter, who seem to have been in the majority, carried the day. As a result, a fundamental change took place in the character of Buddhism and the way of life of the monks. Scholarship came to be considered more important than spiritual practice. Monks who were good scholars came to be more highly esteemed than those who devoted themselves to meditation. As Rahula puts it, 'The solitude-loving meditator lives in seclusion away from society, doing no service to society. The scholar is engaged in service which is necessary for society, and valued by it' (p.27). From the first century BCE, therefore, it is the scholar monk who dominates the scene in Ceylon. The 'rag-robed' monk disappears into the forest, where he exercises less and less influence, and at times even partially adapts himself to the new trends. Eventually, though this the author does not tell us — perhaps because he does not consider the matter important enough, — the practical knowledge of meditation virtually died out in Ceylon and had to be reintroduced from Burma and Thailand in the twentieth century.

7. Study and Meditation: Academic Developments

Scholarship having come to be considered more important than spiritual practice, two separate and mutually exclusive monastic vocations came into existence. A monk could be either a scholar or a meditator, but he could not be both. More extraordinary still, meditation was considered suited to the weak and incapable. 'Able and intelligent *bhikkhus* who were strong in body and mind followed the vocation of scholarship, while *bhikkhus* of weaker intelligence, feeble in body and mind — particularly those who had entered the order in their old age — followed the vocation of meditation (*vipassanā-dhura*)' (p. 30). By the time of King Mahinda IV, in the tenth century CE, the salary paid to the teacher of the *Abhidhamma Piṭaka*, which was 'conducive to the advancement of knowledge', was equal to that of the two teachers of the *Vinaya* and *Sutta Piṭakas*, which were traditionally held to deal with monastic discipline and meditation respectively. With incentives of this sort being offered them, it is not astonishing that monks who took up the vocation of scholarship should have widened their scope to include the various branches of secular knowledge. In this way the whole field of secular education came into the hands of these monks, who enjoyed a comfortable and lucrative existence. They even took up medicine and law. At the end of the chapter Rahula is able to record with satisfaction that as early as the first century CE an elder monk held a post equal to that of Chief Justice of Ceylon. The scholarly monks had clearly become what Coleridge called a *clerisy*, and a Buddhist clerisy is no more the Sangha than a Christian clerisy is the Church.

8. Monasteries: Their Administration and Maintenance

As a result of the educational and other services rendered by the monks to the nation, the monasteries became extremely wealthy. So much so, indeed, that special departments of state had to be created to administer the monasteries and their landed estates, which often included whole villages. The possession of such wealth was not without its disadvantages. Whenever law and order broke down the monasteries had to pay to robbers and bandit chiefs what can only be described as protection money, a practice that eventually came to be regarded with approval. The monasteries also owned large numbers of slaves, both male and female. As Walpola Rahula frankly admits, all this constituted a radical departure from the way of life prescribed for the monks by the Buddha, so much so, indeed, that what he disingenuously calls 'a new monastic way of life' (p. 39) developed in Ceylon. Not that the change seems to bother him particularly. As he says, 'It was the natural result of the inevitable changing political, economic, and social conditions of the country from time to time' (p. 39). The chapter concludes on a curious note. The author finds it difficult to believe that the monks were given so large a portion of the national wealth solely for religious reasons. They were treated so generously, he believes, because they 'worked for the common welfare of the people and the cultural advancement of their country' (p. 39).

9. Arts, Crafts, and Literature

This chapter strikes a happier note. From the 4th century CE onwards the monks of Ceylon not only greatly encouraged the visual arts but themselves sometimes practised them, particularly painting and sculpture. Monks also played an important part in the development of secular literature. Mahanama, in the 5th century CE, composed the *Mahāvaṃsa* or 'Great Chronicle', our principal source for the early history of the island. This work consists mainly of stories about kings, ministers, bandits, wars and rebellions, towns, cities, and countries, all of which are subjects that the Buddha had said it was improper for monks to discuss. Mahanama gets round the difficulty in a highly ingenious manner. By concluding with a reference to death and impermanence, to which even kings are subject, he could claim that each chapter had been converted from a description of worldly affairs into a meditation on the sublime truths of the Dharma. The use of such a device, though innocent in itself, well illustrates the ingenuity with which the Ceylon monk often sought to combine extreme unfaithfulness to the spirit of the Buddha's teaching with scrupulous regard for its letter.

10. National Freedom and the Protection of Peace

Here we see the monks of Ceylon busy with all kinds of political activities. From the 5th to the 18th century they depose and enthrone kings, approve declarations of war, settle feuds, answer questions on the constitution, and negotiate trade pacts. Apart from allowing King Parakrama Bahu the Great to send an army to India to spread 'the Right Faith', they used their vast influence in a humane and moderate manner, and seem to have well deserved the tribute which Rahula pays them for their zeal and prudence.

11. The Portuguese Period

The Portuguese arrived in Ceylon in 1505, at a time of political disintegration, and ruled the maritime provinces from then until 1658. Throughout the territories under their control Roman Catholicism was propogated with fire and sword, and many people embraced the new faith. In the kingdom of Kandy, still ruled by a Sinhalese monarch, the situation was if anything even worse. King Rajasimha I not only gave up Buddhism for Hinduism but behaved with great brutality, killing many *bhikkhus* and burning a large number of religious books. So great was the havoc, that the monastic order ceased to exist, and had to be reintroduced from Arakan at the beginning of the following century. Despite the uninterrupted patronage it had received for centuries, it seems to have collapsed with remarkable ease.

12. The Dutch Period

The Dutch ruled the maritime provinces from 1658 to 1796. Though there was sixty years of peace at the beginning of this period, on the whole the presence of the Dutch was as disastrous to the political, economic, and cultural life of the country as that of the Portuguese had been. So far as the unfortunate inhabitants of the occupied territories were concerned, the only difference was that instead of being forcibly converted to Roman Catholicism they were now forcibly converted to Protestantism. Twice the monastic order died out and twice it had to be reintroduced, once — for the second time — from Arakan, and once from Siam (Thailand). On each occasion the reintroduction seems to have consisted in little more than the restoration of the technically correct tradition of bhikkhu ordination. Despite the noble personality of Saranamkara, who eventually became head of the revived Sangha, there was no question of spiritual renewal. The clerisy re-formed its scattered ranks, and clung on to whatever patronage was still available.

13. British Rule

In 1796 the British conquered the maritime provinces from the Dutch, and in 1815 they gained control of the kingdom of Kandy, thus becoming 'the first and the only foreign power in history to occupy the whole of Ceylon' (p. 64). The author relates a story to show how, on the sad day when the Kandyan Convention was signed, 'the honour and prestige of the Sinhalese and their religion was saved and protected by a *bhikkhu*' (p. 64). This enables him to conclude that 'On every occasion when both the nation and the religion were in danger, Buddhist monks came forward to protect them' (p. 65). However, though otherwise meticulous in citing sources, he gives no authority for his story.

14. Struggle for Freedom: Rebellions

In this chapter we find Buddhist monks assisting, and even leading, armed rebellions against British rule. One elder monk was, indeed, shot on suspicion of complicity in one of these rebellions. 'In the 19th century, as in the past, patriotic Sinhalese laymen and the clergy fought together, sacrificing their lives in the cause of freedom and religion' (p. 67).

15. The Strength of the Bhikkhus: Lay-Clergy Unity

16. British Tactics: Disruption of the Lay-Clergy Unity

17. British Tactics: Confusion of Monastic Administration

18. British Tactics: Intrigues to Destroy Buddhism (Christian Education)

In this group of chapters the author describes the way in which the British disrupted the unity and solidarity of the *bhikkhus* and the laity, won over some of the most prominent elder monks, severed the Government's connection with the administration of Buddhist temporalities, and spread Christianity and Christian culture throughout the country. Article 5 of the Kandyan Convention had declared that 'The Religion of Boodhoo . . . is declared inviolable, and its Rights, Ministers, and Places of Worship are to be maintained and protected,' but this was not observed in the spirit, and hardly in the letter. Indeed, in 1816, the year after the signing of the Convention, we find Governor Sir Robert Brownrigg, in a letter to William Wilberforce, protesting against the suspicion that the word 'inviolable' was being understood in an 'anti-Christian' sense in Ceylon, and assuring his correspondent that the chief object of his Government had been the religious and moral improvement of people, and the propogation of the Gospel (p. 87). For some years the salaries of all Christian missionaries were paid out of the civil list, which meant that Sinhalese Buddhists were having to finance the cost of their own conversion to Christianity! Measures of this sort, which were aimed at the destruction of Buddhism and the enfeeblement of the Sinhalese nation, understandably arouse Walpola Rahula's indignation — an honest indignation that will be shared by all who cherish the ideals of national self-determination and religious tolerance. His harshest strictures, however, are reserved for the chief high priests of the Malvata and Asgiriya Chapters, who on appointment to office undertook to be 'loyal and faithful' to the Government, as well as to report any subversive activities that came to their notice. Such conduct might not have been very heroic, but the author adduces no evidence to show that they necessarily acted from unworthy motives. Perhaps he does not consider it necessary to do so, religio-national patriotism being for him obviously the highest of all virtues.

19. National and Religious Degeneration

With the spread of Christianity and Western education Sinhalese Buddhist culture came to be neglected and despised, even by the Sinhalese Buddhists themselves. The position of the *bhikkhus* deteriorated. As they 'could not adapt themselves to suit the changed political, economic, and social situation, they were rendered useless to society' and 'laymen had nothing to learn from them' (p. 91). Worse still, the Buddhist monk was 'driven to limit his activities to the recitation of the *Suttas* (*Pirit* chanting), preaching a sermon, attendance at funeral rites and almsgiving in memory of the departed, and to an idle, cloistered life in the temple' (p.91). Some Buddhists would probably feel that such activities as chanting and preaching were not altogether unworthy of a Buddhist monk, but Ven. Rahula seems to think that for someone who had been used to enthroning and deposing kings they represent a great come down in the world, and he speaks bitterly of the 'melancholy and abject situation' of such a monk. More extraordinary still, he refers with approval to the ancient Sinhalese idea that a Sinhalese had to be a Buddhist! This is surely a complete denial of the individual's freedom to follow the religion of his own choice, and as such a complete negation of both the spirit and the letter of the Buddha's teaching. One cannot be a Buddhist unless one is free not to be a Buddhist — unless one is free to be a Christian, or a Muslim, or a tree-worshipper, or anything else one wants to be. What Walpola Rahula in effect does is to turn Buddhism from a universal religion into an ethnic religion, surely the worst of all betrayals, the worst of all perversions, of a teaching that stressed above all others the responsibility of the individual for his own development. Indeed, had Walpola Rahula been around at the time of Mahinda's arrival in Ceylon, he probably would have objected to the introduction of the new faith, on the grounds that it was of Indian origin, and would have exhorted the Sinhalese people to remain true to their own traditions. At the end of the chapter he says that 'what the Sinhalese Buddhists opposed was not the religious teaching of Jesus of Nazareth, but a religion together with an alien civilization propogated by the imperialists as a mode of destroying patriotism and notional culture, and re-establishing foreign rule in Ceylon' (p.92). But this does not really help him very much. It was undoubtedly right for the Ceylon Buddhists to resist the forces of Christian religio-imperialism, but what if a Sinhalese wanted to adopt, of his own free will, 'the religious teaching of Jesus of Nazareth'? According to Ven. Rahula, he is not free to do so. He is a Sinhalese and he must be a Buddhist. Moreover, if the Christian missionaries did not represent 'the religious teaching of Jesus of Nazareth' neither did the *bhikkhus* of Ceylon — at least those with whom Rahula is concerned — represent the religious teaching of Gautama of Kapilavastu. Rahula does not understand this. He does not understand that what really happened during the period of British rule, if it had not happened even earlier, was that the Christian clerisy, as represented by the missionaries, to a large extent superseded the Buddhist clerisy as represented by the monks. The more powerful 'medicine' of the West virtually ousted the weaker 'medicine' of the East. Quoting Rahula's own words in an earlier chapter one might say that this was an example, on an even wider and historically more important scale, of 'the inevitable changing political, economic, and social conditions' in the world. In fact, what took place was not so much a clash between Buddhism and Christianity, or even a clash between Buddhism and the forces of religio-imperialism, but a clash between two rival clerisies. Buddhism as a living spiritual tradition had disappeared from Ceylon long before the British came. What collapsed under the combined impact of Christianity and Western education was the clerisy, and it is degeneration in this sense that Rahula is really lamenting in this chapter.

20. The Revival

Just as degeneration was the degeneration of the clerisy, so revival was the revival of the clerisy. From 1841 onwards *pirivenas* or Buddhist monastic institutes for the study of the traditional learning and culture were established, Buddhist schools were opened, and Buddhist societies founded. However, reading between the lines of Rahula's account, it is clear that 'revival' tended to mean two quite different things. In the first place it meant the revival of the traditional learning and culture. In the second it meant the teaching of Western arts and sciences under 'Buddhist' auspices. Thus there were, in fact, now two clerisies, one consisting of those Buddhist monks who had been educated at the *pirivenas*, and one consisting of those laymen — and monks too, eventually — who had received a Western education. As a result of this, the conflict between the 'Christian' clerisy and the 'Buddhist' clerisy was reproduced within the Sinhalese Buddhist community itself. One interesting development of this conflict was that many of the wealthy, Western-educated Sinhalese Buddhists not only sent their children to Christian missionary schools (presumably because they believed Western 'medicine' to be superior to Eastern 'medicine') but believed that *bhikkhus* 'ought to confine themselves to purely religious activities and,' in Rahula's own words, 'live a life limited to the four walls of their temples' (p. 95). Rahula believes that such wealthy laymen wanted to keep the *bhikkhus* out of politics for purely selfish reasons, and with regard to some of them he is undoubtedly right. At the same time it ought to be considered that some laymen of this class, being themselves members of the dominant clerisy, looked to the members of the monastic order for something more than just learning and culture — for a higher, 'spiritual' something that neither the Christian missionaries nor the 'political' *bhikkhus* possessed. Where a need of this sort is concerned, however, Rahula seems quite unsympathetic, even uncomprehending. *Bhikkhus* ignorant of the modern world and its problems he dismisses as 'a set of meaningless ancients' (p. 96). His ideal is represented by the knowledgeable and energetic *bhikkhus* of the present generation who, he declares, have no wish to chant *pirit*, perform funeral rites, or deliver 'the usual sermons'. Such *bhikkhus* have 'considered it their duty and heritage once again to liberate their country, nation, and religion' and this, according to him, is 'the inevitable course of history which cannot be stopped' (p. 97).

On this stirring note *The Heritage of the Bhikkhu* ends. Since its original appearance in Sinhalese in 1946, however, a great deal has happened in Sri Lanka, and Walpola Rahula has therefore added to this English edition of his famous book a postscript which brings the story down to 1971, the year of the great insurgency. In 1948 Ceylon became independent. Those who had assumed that the end of foreign rule would mean automatic reversion to full-fledged religio-nationalism were however soon disappointed. Whether or not the process of history cannot be stopped, Rahula and his friends had certainly miscalculated its direction. Nevertheless, such was the enthusiasm for national, cultural, and religious revival that, in the first decade after independence, it seemed as though a veritable renaissance was taking place. A World Fellowship of Buddhists was inaugurated, a Buddhist council held, a Buddhist Committee of Inquiry appointed, and the 2500th Buddha Jayanti celebrated on a grand scale throughout the country. At the same time, the *bhikkhus* became more deeply involved in social reform and welfare activities of various kinds, while among both monks and laymen there was a growing demand for the implementation of the recommendations of the Buddhist Committee of Inquiry, which had proposed widespread changes, and the declaration of Sinhalese as the national language. This demand was spearheaded by the 'political' bhikkhus, and with their support the Sri Lanka Freedom Party, which had promised to implement the Committee's proposals, won the General Election of 1956. For a while it seemed as though the wildest dreams of religio-nationalism were about to become a reality. Then in 1958 the Prime Minister, Mr S. R. W. D. Bandaranaike, was assassinated by a Buddhist monk. I was in India at the time and I well remember the sensation the news created. 'Generally speaking', Rahula tells us, 'the *bhikkhus* could not face the public for several years' (p. 109). In the light of what Rahula has told us about the *bhikkhu* 'in educational, cultural, social, and political life' throughout the centuries it now seems, in retrospect, that sooner or later a tragedy of this sort was bound to take place. Indeed assassination, or attempted assassination, was part of the heritage of the *bhikkhu* in Ceylon. In a curious footnote, Rahula tells us that in the first century CE about sixty *bhikkhus* who had attempted to assassinate the king were executed by being thrown over a high rock (p. 161). When the *bhikkhus* again 'faced the public' and appeared on the political scene, at the time of the 1965 General Election, their forces were divided. Some supported the United National Party, which carried the day, and some the SLFP, which went back into opposition. 'Thus,' Rahula concludes with satisfaction, '*bhikkhus* on both sides were again in the forefront' (p. 109).

Again in the forefront! These words contain a clue to

much that is muddled in Rahula's thinking, and much, indeed, that is ambiguous in his own position. To him it does not matter, apparently, if *bhikkhus* campaign for rival political parties — and from what I remember from newspaper reports at the time the campaigning was not conducted in a very gentlemanly fashion. What matters is that they should take a prominent part in whatever happens to be going on. In other words. The *bhikkhu* — or rather the 'political' *bhikkhu* — like his 'socially' oriented counterpart in the modern 'Christian' West — is in fact *looking for a role*. Two thousand years ago he lost faith in Buddhism as a path of individual spiritual development and gave up being a monk in the original, more 'spiritual' sense of the term to become a member of the Buddhist clerisy. This gave him both influence and prestige and for some centuries he was satisfied. Now, however, the 'Buddhist' clerisy has been superseded by a secular, modern clerisy to whom he has forfeited much of his former position in society and with whom he is increasingly compelled to compete on equal terms. The results of this are to be seen in the second decade after independence. Losing all contact with Buddhism as a path of individual development, the 'political' *bhikkhus* lose their separate identity and become submerged in the mainstream of secular political life. Eventually, in the mass insurgency that followed the failure of the United Left Front to honour its election promises, 'hundreds of *bhikkhus* were arrested, humiliated, tortured, or killed' (p. 117).

Going through Ven. Rahula's celebrated essay (based, he tells us, on a speech given in Kandy in 1946), it should not be forgotten that his reading of the history of Buddhism in Ceylon is a somewhat selective one, and that even in Ceylon the heritage of the *bhikkhu* is not so exclusively political and cultural as he would have us believe. 'Rag-robed', forest-dwelling monks seem to have existed at all periods, and in recent times there has even been a revival of interest in meditation. Nevertheless, there is no doubt that the account which he gives is substantially correct, and that religio-nationalism is the dominant feature of the Buddhism of Ceylon. There is no doubt, either, that Rahula himself is deeply committed to this trend. Indeed, one of the most remarkable features of the whole book is his entire unconsciousness of the more spiritual, transcendental aspects of the Dharma. For Rahula these simply do not exist. He knows about them as a scholar, of course, but it is clear that for him they are only ideas, only words, and mean nothing to him personally. With the spiritual life a closed book, and religio-nationalism in a state of collapse, he is indeed in a strange position, being left with the purely scholarly work for which he is, of course, now best known.

In an interesting appendix, Rahula argues that patriotism is not necessarily the last refuge of a scoundrel, and that politics, understood as disinterested participation in public life, is not incompatible with the religious life - indeed, may even be an expression of it. Even though they may agree with this in principle, however, most Western Buddhists will put the book down with an overwhelming impression that the heritage of the *bhikkhu*, as described by Rahula, is a heritage of shame. With its record of almost continuous betrayal of the spirit of the Buddha's teaching it provides us with a saddening and sickening example of what happens when ultimate spiritual objectives are replaced by secondary cultural and political ones — when a universal religion is transmogrified into an ethnic one and the spiritual community becomes a cultural elite. It is therefore a heritage with which I for one want as little as possible to do. What our *real* heritage is, in both East and West, is for me sufficiently indicated by the Buddha, when he declared, 'O monks, ye are mine own true sons, born of my mouth, born of the Dharma. Therefore, O monks, be ye heirs of the Dharma, not heirs of worldly things'.

The White Lotus Sutra in the West*

The *Saddharma Puṇḍarīka* or 'White Lotus-flower of the True Doctrine' *Sutra* is one of the oldest and most important of the Mahayana sutras. Cited by the Indian master Nagarjuna, who flourished towards the end of the first century CE, as a literary composition it belongs essentially to the first century BCE and thus is contemporaneous with the Pali Tipiṭaka, which was also committed to writing at about this time. The Sutra is important for a number of reasons. Doctrinally speaking, it is important mainly on account of its two fundamental teachings, both of which, after being distinctly enunciated for the first time in this sutra, became an integral part of the basic structure of Mahayana thought and practice. According to the first of these teachings, there is ultimately only one yana, the Buddhayana, which leads to Buddhahood. The Buddha speaks of two yanas, or three yanas, simply as an expedient device in order to help those of lesser spiritual attainments who, for the time being at least, are aiming at inferior goals. Eventually, all beings will come into the One Way and all will attain Buddhahood. According to the second of these two teachings, the Buddha's span of life is infinite. He is in truth neither born nor passes away into final Nirvana, both of these acts being only appearances,

---

*Tripitaka Master Tu Lun *The Essentials of the Dharma Blossom Sutra* Volume 1. Translated by Bhikshu Heng Ch'ien (San Francisco, California: Buddhist Text Translation Society, 1974)

only expedient devices for the benefit of the less spiritually developed. The Sutra is also important for its literary form. Unlike some Mahayana sutras, it has a definite structure, almost dramatic in character, which remains more or less intact despite the apparent incorporation, at a later date, of extraneous, or at least not very directly related, material. But the great glory of the *White Lotus Sutra* are its parables. These include the parables of the Burning House, the Raincloud, the 'Prodigal Son', the Magic City, and many others. Closely connected with the Sutra's importance as literature is its importance for art. In China and Japan particularly, scenes from the Sutra — like that in which Sakyamuni, having opened the miraculously-appearing Stupa and revealed the 'extinct' Buddha Prabhutaratna, takes his seat on one half of the latter's lion-throne — were frequently depicted in both painting and sculpture, as a result of which the message of the Sutra became more and more widely known, even outside specifically Buddhist circles. Historically speaking, the *White Lotus Sutra* is important because of the high esteem in which it was held by the eclectic and philosophical T'ien T'ai School, which with the possible exception of the Hua-yen or Avatamsaka School, is probably the most representative and influential school of Chinese Buddhism. According to this school, the *White Lotus Sutra* is the Buddha's ultimate teaching, delivered during the last phase of his earthly career, and it has been the subject of profound and systematic study by the third patriarch and virtual founder of the school, Chi-i (or Chih-ke), as well as by numerous other masters of the T'ien T'ai lineage.

In modern times, the *Saddharma Puṇḍarīka* was one of the first Buddhist scriptures to be translated into a European language. The Sanskrit text having been brought from Nepal earlier in the century, it was translated into French by Eugene Burnouf as early as 1852. Some years later, in

1884, came the first English translation. This appeared as Volume 21 in the famous 'Sacred Books of the East' series, edited by F. Max Muller, and was the work of the Dutch orientalist Hendrik Kern. Bearing in mind that in those days there was little sympathy in the world of oriental scholarship for Buddhism as a spiritual teaching, and that its technical vocabulary was hardly understood at all, Kern's translation is a good pioneer attempt, even though its pages are frequently marred by footnotes in which he tries to prove that the Buddha was a solar myth. Perhaps unfortunately, Kern's translation is even now the one in which the *White Lotus Sutra* is most widely known in the English speaking world, it having been reprinted several times. After Kern came W. E. Soothill, who in collaboration with the Japanese scholar Bunno Kato produced an English version of the Sutra based on Kumarajiva's Chinese translation, made in 406 CE. Soothill's version, which was published in an abridged form in 1930 as *The Sutra of the Lotus of the Wonderful Law*, is much easier reading than Kern's, being in fact altogether more poetic and inspiring. Though an ex-missionary, and a professor at Oxford, Soothill was highly appreciative of the religious and 'apocalyptic' elements in the Sutra, and did his best to do full justice to these, though the profounder, more 'philosophical' content of the Sutra tends to escape him. After Soothill little happened for forty years to make the *White Lotus Sutra* more accessible to the English speaking world. In 1962 there appeared Conze's translation of the Sanskrit text of Chapter 5, 'On Plants', and that was all. English and American Buddhists and students of Buddhism, who meanwhile had greatly increased in number, — especially since the end of the war, — remained dependent for their knowledge of one of the greatest and most important of all Buddhist scriptures either on Kern's unattractive and sometimes misleading translation or on

Soothill's more readable but incomplete version. Since the beginning of the present decade the situation has changed, and due to the efforts of Chinese, Japanese, and American Buddhists, it is now possible for us to have a better understanding of the Sutra in the West. In 1970 the Kosei Publishing Company, Tokyo, brought out a revised version of the complete Soothill/Kato translation, while in 1975 this version reappeared under the Weatherill/Kosei imprint together with translations of 'The Sutra of Innumerable Meanings', and 'The Sutra of Meditation on the Bodhisattva Universal Virtue' as *The Threefold Lotus Sutra*. Both volumes were meticulously edited and beautifully produced. A year earlier, in 1974, the Buddhist Text Translation Society, San Francisco, had brought out *The Essentials of the Dharma Blossom Sutra*, Volume 1, by the Chinese Tripitaka Master Tu Lun, and it is with this that we are now concerned.

According to the Short Biography of the Master which is appended to the volume, Ven. Tu Lun was born in north-eastern China in 1908. Becoming a shramanera or novice monk at the age of 19, after his mother's death, he lived in solitude for a while and practised meditation. After the Second World War he was ordained as a bhikshu or full monk, and travelled south to pay his respects to the Venerable Master Hsu Yun, then 109 years old. In 1950 he left for Hong Kong, where for the benefit of refugee monks from the mainland he helped establish monasteries and temples throughout the island. In 1962 he arrived in San Francisco, and there from 1968 to 1970 delivered the lectures on which *The Essentials of the Dharma Blossom Sutra* is based. This work, which has been edited and translated by the Master's American disciple Bhikshu Heng Ch'ien (David Fox), will be complete in three volumes, the second and third of which are yet to come. The work is of special importance for three reasons: (1) It is the first English translation of the *White Lotus Sutra* to be made entirely by believing and practising Buddhists working in the traditional manner, (2) It is the first English translation of the Sutra to be accompanied by a commentary in which the Sutra is explained according to the traditional interpretation of the text, in this case that of the T'ien T'ai School, and (3) It is the first English translation of the Sutra to be made as a result of close collaboration between Eastern and Western Buddhists, especially Tripitaka Master Tu Lun and his disciple Bhikshu Heng Ch'ien.

The present volume consists of the first two chapters of the Sutra, which contains in all twenty-seven or twenty-eight chapters, together with the Master's commentary on each chapter in turn. The text of the Sutra has been translated from Kumarajiva's Chinese version, which is the one generally used in China, and for the convenience of the reader each chapter is printed twice, first in its entirety before the commentary, and again in sections in the body of the commentary. Text and commentary are preceded by a lengthy introduction, as well as by a biography of Kumarajiva. The introduction, which serves to introduce the commentary to the entire Sutra, takes the form of an exposition of the T'ien T'ai School's five-fold discussion of the recondite principles of the Sutra, *viz.* explanation of the title, clarification of the substance, elucidation of the doctrine, discussion of the function, and determination of the teaching. This part of the work gives us a better insight into the teachings of the T'ien T'ai School, and its approach to the White Lotus Sutra, than anything that has yet appeared in English. One stands amazed at the profundity of thought of Chi-i and the other T'ien T'ai masters, and feels deeply grateful to Ven. Tu Lun and Bhikshu Heng Ch'ien for making this thought accessible to us. The commentary itself follows the detailed and highly analytical Outline of the Sutra made by the Ming Dynasty

Dharma Master No-i. Like the introduction, the commentary is rich and varied in content, giving us not only treasures of T'ien T'ai thought but expositions of standard Buddhist teachings, biographies of eminent disciples of the Buddha, pithy sayings, poems, anecdotes from the Master's own experience, and even specimens of Chinese Buddhist folklore. Particularly noteworthy are the Master's exposition of the portent of shaking the earth (pp. 199-201), his discussion of the eight *vimokṣas* or 'liberations', here called the eight renunciations (pp. 337-340), as well as the whole of the introduction to Chapter 1, 'Expedient Devices', in which the Master explains the interdependency of the provisional and actual teachings and points out how, in the context of this chapter, 'expedient device' has the specific meaning of opening up the provisional teaching to reveal the actual. On a somewhat different level, there is an interesting reference to the Buddha's age on leaving home and on gaining Enlightenment. Following a well-known Pali verse, in which the Buddha himself is represented as speaking, one usually says that the Buddha left home at the age of twenty-nine and gained Enlightenment six years later at the age of thirty-five. Ven. Tu Lun, however, presumably following ancient Indian traditions translated from Sanskrit into Chinese, says of the Buddha, 'He left the palace and all its pleasures at the age of nineteen to cultivate the Way and realized Buddhahood at the age of thirty' (p. 108). This would seem to agree with texts like the Pabbajjā-sutta of the *Sutta-nipāta*, one of the more ancient 'books' of the Pali Canon, which give the definite impression that the future Buddha must have left home at a considerably earlier age than twenty-nine. There is also the curious story of the delayed birth of the Buddha's son Rahula. Again presumably following ancient Indian tradition, Ven. Tu Lun tells us that on his father's demanding a grandson from him before he would permit him to leave the home-life, 'Sakyamuni Buddha merely pointed a finger at the belly of his wife, Yasodhara, and told her that in six years time she would bear a son' (p. 154). The master goes on to remark that this may seem rather incredible, but that in the Buddhadharma there are a great many mysteries more profound. No doubt there are, but is it not possible that the story of Rahula's delayed birth arose in order to reconcile the fact that he had been born after the Buddha's departure from home with the 'fact' that, according to the accepted account, the Buddha's departure had taken place some years later than it actually had done? The whole question awaits further investigation, and the key to its solution may well be found in the traditions on which Ven. Tu Lun has drawn. Meanwhile, we had best keep an open mind on the subject, and perhaps accustom ourselves to the idea of a quite youthful Buddha.

Though there is much else in this invaluable work that invites comment, in a short review it is hardly possible to do justice to the wealth of material that Ven. Tu Lun and Bhikshu Heng Ch'ien have placed at our disposal. Enough has been said, I hope, to show that the publication of *The Essentials of the Dharma Blossom Sutra* marks the beginning of a new era in the study and appreciation of this sutra in the West. Even when the two remaining volumes have been brought out, however, much will still remain to be done. The *White Lotus Sutra* will be fully known and appreciated in the West only when four conditions have been fulfilled: (1) There must be a new English translation of the Sanskrit text of the Sutra. This should be both accurate and inspiring, doing full justice to the doctrinal terminology and poetic imagery alike. Dr Conze's rendering of Chapter 5, 'On Plants', is a step in the right direction, and it is to be hoped that either Dr Conze himself or a scholar of equal ability will soon provide us with a comparable version of the remainder of the Sutra. Bhikshu Heng Ch'ien's version of the gatha portion of the Sutra is in the same short, breathless lines as Soothill's, only more regularly stressed, and though on the whole admirably clear, direct, and vigorous its language is not only less polished than Soothill's but even, at times, quite rough and clumsy. (2) We must have at our disposal all the traditional interpretations of the *White Lotus Sutra*. Though the Indian master Vasubandhu is said to have written a commentary on the Sutra, this appears to have been lost, and we therefore have to rely mainly on the expositions of Chinese and Japanese masters, especially those of the T'ien T'ai School. (3) The Sutra must be studied directly, in the light of what we know about the historical development of Buddhism, as well as studied in the light of traditional expositions, and the real nature of its teaching ascertained. It will also be necessary to examine the relation between that teaching and (a) the total Buddhist tradition, and (b) Western thought. Ven. Tu Lun's approach to the Sutra is 'fundamentalist', but for the Western Buddhist, aware as he usually is that the tradition represented by Ven. Tu Lun is not the only one in the Buddhist world, such an attitude is not possible — or possible only at the sacrifice of some of the very qualities on which the pursuit of the spiritual life itself depends. But not to be fundamentalist is not to be untraditional, much less still unBuddhistic. We have to adopt towards the vast mass of material that has poured into the West from all over the Buddhist world the same approach that Chi-i, in the fifth century CE, adopted towards the material that had flooded into China from India and Central Asia. What we need is a new, updated T'ien T'ai School! (4) The teaching of the Sutra must be related to the concrete spiritual needs of Western Buddhists. However sublime a teaching may be, it is virtually meaningless unless it is able to bring about a radical transformation in the lives of individual human beings.

These four conditions will probably not be fulfilled for some time to come. Meanwhile, in *The Essentials of the Dharma Blossom Sutra* we have a major contribution to the fulfilment of at least the second of them, and the appearance of the second and third volumes of the work will therefore be eagerly awaited.

Zen Past and Present*

According to tradition, Zen began when the Buddha held up a golden flower in the midst of the assembly. No one understood the meaning of his action except Mahakashyapa, who smiled. The Buddha thereupon declared, 'This is the profound and mysterious principle of Enlightenment, which I now transmit to you, O Mahakashyapa!' In this way the Dharma was transmitted to Mahakashyapa, who thereupon became the first Zen patriarch. It was transmitted not through the medium of words, nor even through the medium of thoughts, but directly, from mind to mind, or from heart to heart, by a process of what may be called transcendental telepathy. Emphasizing this aspect of Zen, a traditional Chinese verse speaks of it as 'A special transmission outside the Scriptures; No dependence on words and letters'. Nonetheless, despite its claim to be a 'wordless', purely spiritual transmission of the Buddha's 'Teaching', and its

*The Blue Cliff Record, volume 1. Translated from the Chinese Pi Yen Lu by Thomas and J. C. Cleary. Foreword by Taizan Maezumi Roshi (Boulder & London: Shambhala, 1977)

Irmgard Schloegl The Zen Way (London: Sheldon, 1977)

Thomas Merton on Zen (London: Sheldon, 1976)

Bhagwan Shree Rajneesh No Water No Moon: Reflections on Zen (London:Sheldon, 1977)

Trevor Leggett The Tiger's Cave: Translations of Japanese Zen Texts (London & Henley: Routledge & Kegan Paul, 1977)

apparent aversion to scriptural studies, in the course of more than a thousand years of recognizable historical existence the Zen school produced an enormous quantity of literature, much of it of great literary and spiritual significance, and including works which came to be regarded as being in effect scriptures in their own right. This literature was produced, of course, mainly in Chinese and Japanese. In recent decades a small portion of it has been translated into various European languages, and in this way has come to influence the spiritual lives of a number of people in the West. Besides such translations of the Zen classics, as they may be called, books 'about' Zen have been written by Buddhists and non-Buddhists, Easterners and Westerners, of widely varying degrees of authority and experience. A fairly representative batch of such publications is now before us. It might be useful to look first at the translation of a Zen classic of exceptional importance and then, using this as a sort of touchstone, at the modern works.

The Zen classic in question is the *Pi Yen Lu* or *Blue Cliff Record*, an eleventh century Chinese compilation in one hundred chapters, the first thirty-five of which have now been translated by two American scholars. To review a work of this kind is almost as much out of the question as reviewing a sutra. One could, of course, shout 'Mu!' or threaten the translators and their publishers with thirty blows. Or one could even leave these columns blank by way of registering one's protest against being expected to 'add flowers to brocade' in this way. But much as connoisseurs of Zen might relish such behaviour, it would not be of much help to the ordinary reader. Let us therefore approach the work by way of its literary structure. Essentially it is a collection of one hundred anecdotes of the sayings and doings of the Chinese Ch'an masters and disciples of the 8th to the 10th centuries CE, a period which may be regarded as the Golden Age of Ch'an. These anecdotes were compiled from traditional sources by the Ch'an master Hsueh Tou Ch'ung Hsien (980-1052 CE), who also composed a poem on each anecdote. About sixty years after Hsueh Tou's death another Ch'an master, Yuan Wu K'e Ch'in (1063-1135 CE) gave a series of talks elucidating the anecdotes and the poems. Each chapter of the *Blue Cliff Record* (so called from the name of the temple where Yuan Wu gave his talks) therefore consists of six parts: (1) Yuan Wu's introduction (missing in some cases); (2) the anecdote, taken from Ch'an tradition or Buddhist scripture; (3) remarks by Yuan Wu on certain points in the anecdote; (4) commentary on the anecdote by Yuan Wu; (5) the poem by Hsueh Tou, interspersed with remarks by Yuan Wu, and (6) commentary by Yuan Wu on the poem and its relation to the anecdote.

The nucleus of each chapter is thus the anecdote, to which poem, remark, and commentary were gradually added in a manner resembling the process of accretion that forms a pearl, and it is worth enquiring why this should be so. As noted already, Zen claims to be 'A special transmission outside the scriptures'. In its own terminology, it was the 'school of the patriarchs', that is to say, the school of the living exemplars of Enlightenment, as distinct from the T'ien T'ai and Hua Yen schools, for example, which were 'doctrinal schools', or schools specializing in the systematic study of a certain sutra or group of sutras. This being so, it was hardly possible for the Zen masters to base their teaching on systematic expositions of the scriptures. They therefore developed the practice of taking as their starting point something that an earlier Zen master (or other ancient Buddhist worthy) had said or done. Since the master was enlightened, his words or actions would be an expression of the Enlightenment-experience, and therefore able to give the Zen disciple some clue as to what it was all about. They would serve as a spiritual precedent, as it were, by which the validity of his own attainment could be tested. In this way originated the *kung an* (Chinese) or *Koan* (Japanese), as the anecdotes which were used in this way came to be called. Literally the term *kung an* means a 'public case' or 'public record', that is to say, a legal case which can be cited as a precedent for the settlement of new cases. The *Blue Cliff Record* is therefore essentially a collection of koans, complete with examples of the way in which these were used by, and the kind of effect they had on, subsequent generations of masters and disciples of the most spiritually vital and creative period in Ch'an history — which is to say, one of the most spiritually vital and creative periods in the entire history of Buddhism. The purpose of the koans was to function as catalysts of Enlightenment. As Yuan Wu says, 'Whenever the Ancients handed down a word or half a phrase, it was like sparks struck from flint, like a flash of lightning, directly opening up a single straight path' (p. 47).

The rather complex literary structure of the *Pi Len Yu* made possible the creation of a work of extraordinary richness, variety, and beauty, and in his foreword to the translation Taizan Maezumi Roshi rightly describes it as 'one of the most wonderful dharma-treasures of the world's Eastern heritage' (p. ix). Its hundred 'cases' are, he tells us, equivalent to all the dharmas preached by Shakyamuni Buddha, and each 'case' contains innumerable dharmas. The work is, in fact, a whole world in itself — a world in which, or in even a corner of which, one could well spend one's whole life and hardly notice that the time had passed. In this world — which is the world of T'ang and Sung Dynasty China and yet, at the same time, our own world — we encounter all sorts of wonderful and extraordinary figures, some of whom are already known to Western students of Zen. Apart from semi-legendary figures like Bodhidharma, there is Huang Po, who was seven feet tall, had a lump in his forehead like a round pearl, and who 'understood Ch'an by nature'; Pai Chang, who compiled the so-called 'pure standards' for Zen monasteries, and who first thundered in the scandalized ears of an eleemosynary generation, 'A day of no working is a day of no eating'; the nun Iron Grindstone Liu, who had studied for a long time, and whose active edge was 'sharp and dangerous'; and Yun Men, to whose lineage belonged both Hsieh Tou and Yuan Wu. Yun Men liked to teach three word Ch'an. He also taught one word Ch'an. In ordinary situations, even, he would revile people. 'When he uttered a phrase it was like an iron spike' (p. 39). Hsiang Lin Teng Yuan, one of the 'Four Sages', served as Yun Men's attendant for eighteen years. Whenever Yun Men dealt with him, he would just call out, 'Attendant Yuan!' Yuan would answer 'Yes?' Yun Men would say, 'What is it?' It went on like this for eighteen years, when one day Hsiang Lin finally awakened. We also meet Master Chu Ti, who whenever anything was asked would just raise one finger; Ma Tsu, famous for polishing a rock in order to make it into a mirror; and Chao Chu, who awakened to the way when he was nearly 60, settled down at a temple at 80, and taught until his death at 120. He was also known for his asceticism. 'When one leg of his rope chair broke, he tied on a leftover piece of firewood with rope to support it. There were repeated requests to make a new leg for it, but the master would not allow it' (p. 228). We hear, too, Tung Shan's celebrated 'Three pounds of hemp', see the hermit of Lotus Flower Peak holding up his staff, and listen to the dialogue between Manjushri and Wu Cho.

The world of the *Blue Cliff Record* is in fact a world in which we encounter no one except masters and disciples, all of whom are concerned with nothing except

Enlightenment. 'When the ancients travelled on foot to visit the monasteries everywhere', says Yuan Wu, 'they only had this matter on their minds; they wanted to discern whether the old teacher on the carved wooden seat possessed eyes or did not possess eyes' (p. 195). For 'patch-robed monks' of this kind, who spent the greater part of their lives trudging the roads of China or meditating on remote mountain peaks, Zen was not a matter of 'the witty word among the tea-cups' (as a correspondent once described the London based Zen of the 'fifties) but literally a matter of life and death. Yun Men went to see Mu Chou. 'As soon as he opened the door a little, (Yun Men) immediately bounded in; Mu Chou held him fast and said, 'Speak! Speak!' Yun Men hesitated, and was pushed out; he still had one foot inside when Mu Chou slammed the door, breaking Yun Men's leg. As Yun Men cried out in pain, he was suddenly greatly enlightened' (pp. 37-38). In a word, the world of the *Blue Cliff Record* is a world in which *Buddhism matters*, — is the only thing that matters, — and in which people are prepared to go to any lengths in order to attain — and transmit — 'the profound and mysterious principle of Enlightenment'.

In introducing us to this world, so strange and yet so familiar, the translators of the *Pi Yen Lu* have widened our spiritual horizons immeasurably, and given us access to an inexhaustible treasure. As they state in their introduction, 'The publication of *The Blue Cliff Record* in English will help open new vistas in the study of Buddhism in the West,' — even though it is true that this is, in their own modest words, 'only part of a larger task' (p. xxiii). What effect these new vistas will have on the spiritual lives of American and English Buddhists, and on the course of Western Buddhism, it is impossible to predict. There is little doubt, however, that this classic of Zen literature will not be used in quite the same way as in ancient China or modern Japan, and that its influence will not be confined to 'official' Zen circles. There is also little doubt that, when the two remaining volumes are published, this version of the *Blue Cliff Record* will take its place with Rhys Davids's 'Dialogues of the Buddha' and Conze's 'Perfection of Wisdom' as a major contribution to our knowledge of the primary sources of Buddhist tradition.

From the Zen classic of the eleventh century CE to the modern works 'about' Zen is nearly a thousand years, and it would not be strange if something of the spirit of Zen had evaporated in the interim. The author of *The Zen Way*, Irmgard Schloegl, has at least spent twelve years in Japan undergoing traditional Zen training, and her chapter on 'Training in a Japanese Zen Monastery', a fascinating account of the whole cycle of the monastic year, will certainly dispel a few illusions. Though life in a Zen monastery is hard, and discipline strict, Dr Schloegl is at pains to show that the human element is not lacking, and that even head monks have hearts of gold. Valuable as this chapter is, however, the real substance of the book is to be found in the short introduction and the chapters entitled 'Fundamentals' and 'Application'. For Dr Schloegl the Zen Way is above all a way of training that has as its object the genuine transformation — not merely the sublimation — of primitive emotional energy. It is this energy which is traditionally spoken of as the 'heart' (not 'mind', she insists) of man, and which is symbolized by the 'splendid, tremendously strong, powerful, wild, and quite ungovernable bull' of the well known bull-herding pictures. In dealing with the practical side of the transformation process, clearly her central concern, Dr Schloegl rightly emphasizes that primitive emotions should be neither repressed nor expressed, and well shows how the disciplined life of the Zen monastery helps the monk to achieve the middle way in this respect. She is also alive to the danger of what she terms 'siezure', which occurs when a man is carried away by untransformed emotional energy, as well as to the related danger of regression, when the unleashed energy turns destructive. In dealing with the theoretical implications of the transformation process she is less reliable. Her grasp of Buddhist doctrine is, in fact, at times distinctly shaky. Yet even though her active edge may not be as sharp and dangerous as Iron Grindstone Liu's it is certainly formidable enough to deal with anything she is likely to find in the neighbourhood of Eccleston Square.

I have only one real criticism. In the absence of temples and training monasteries Dr Schloegl suggests that we in the West should take our ordinary daily life (i.e. job, housework) as our training discipline. This is, of course, something that could well be done — indeed, in principle should be done. In making the suggestion, however, Dr Schloegl appears to overlook two things: (1) The extent to which modern economic life violates the principles of Right Livelihood; and (2) The possibility of our going away 'on retreat' from time to time and benefitting from the positively structured routine of a quasi-monastic environment *for a limited period* — as frequently happens in the FWBO. If the routine of ordinary life was sufficient as a training discipline the Buddha would not have founded a monastic order, the masters and disciples of the *Blue Cliff Record* would not have all been monks, and there would have been no Zen monastery for Dr Schloegl herself to stay at when she went to Japan. 'Daily Life Practice' is not the same thing as the acceptance of the status quo.

Thomas Merton was a Roman Catholic monk of the Cistercian Order of Strict Observance (the Trappists) who wrote a great deal about Eastern mysticism, especially Zen. The essays collected in *Thomas Merton on Zen* are a selection from what the publishers call his 'prodigious output'. Some are chapters taken from books which he himself published as such, while others are prefaces to books by other people. In view of the miscellaneous nature of its origin, it would not be fair to review the present collection as though it was a book in the strict sense of the term. Nevertheless it does have a certain unity which allows us to treat it in this way to some extent. This unity is not due to the fact that all the essays are about Zen, or have some bearing on it, nor even to the fact that the author always approaches his subject from the same point of view. It stems, rather, from the nature of the author's own mental makeup as revealed in all these pieces. Thomas Merton is clearly a well read, well informed man of great mental agility and verbal fluency who is ready to define Zen — or anything else — at the drop of a biretta. On page 4 he tells us that 'It is a product of the combination of Mahayana Buddhism with Chinese Taoism which was later transported to Japan and further refined there'. Though what may be called the Mrs Beeton theory of the origin of Zen has enjoyed the support of people who should have known better, even a cursory glance at the first volume of the *Blue Cliff Record* will show us no sign of Mahayana Buddhism in process of being 'combined' with Taoism in this way. One will be lucky if one finds very much 'Mahayana Buddhism'. All one finds is people concerned, either as masters or disciples, with 'this matter'. On page 52 Father Merton returns to the attack. 'Zen is, in fact,' he assures us, 'an Asian form of religious existentialism'. He is equally ready to define — and compare — Zen enlightenment and Rilke's *'nowhere without no'*. 'Zen enlightenment is an insight into being in all its existential reality and actualization. It is a fully alert and superconscious *act* of being which transcends time and space. Such is the attainment of the "Buddha mind" or

"Buddhahood". (Compare the Christian expressions "having the mind of Christ" |1 Corinthians 2.16|, being "of one spirit with Christ", "He who is united to the Lord is one spirit" |1 Corinthians 6. 17|, though the Buddhist idea |sic| takes no account of any supernatural order in the Thomist sense.)' (p. 6). 'That *"Nowhere without no"* (a mysterious expression) is the void of *śūnyatā* |Thanks for telling us!| and the emptiness of Eckhart's "Ground" or, perhaps more properly, Boehme's "Un-ground" (*Ungrund*). "God" says Boheme, "is called the seeing and finding of the Nothing. And it is therefore called a Nothing (though it is God Himself) because it is inconceivable and inexpressible." This is more theological than Rilke . . . ' (p. 78) etc., etc., blah blah blah. Thomas Merton is quite capable of going on like this for pages together. In a famous phrase, he is 'intoxicated with the exuberance of his own verbosity'. Or as Yuan Wu puts it, 'Because later students become attached to their words and more and more give rise to intellectual interpretations, therefore they do not see the Ancients' message' (*The Blue Cliff Record*, p. 57).

This is not to say that there are not good things to be found in these essays. Despite his weakness for 'intellectual interpretations', Father Merton's facility of expression at times enables him to hit the nail firmly and squarely on the head. Speaking of the results of koan study and the identity of 'individuality' and 'desire', for instance, he says, 'It is not as if the "individual" were a hard, substantial, ontological core from which desires proceed, but rather that desires themselves form a kind of knot of psychic energies which seek to remain firmly tied as the autonomous "self" '(p. 74). This could hardly be better put. Nonetheless, the overall impression remains that in these essays Thomas Merton is preoccupied not with Zen so much as with what others have thought and said about Zen. This is not because he was never in Japan.

It is not even because he never actually practised Zen Buddhism. Rather, it is because he was so highly skilled in the manipulation of words and concepts, and became so deeply absorbed in the exercise of that skill, that he was unable to distinguish words and concepts from realities, and when he was playing elaborate games with the one thought he was dealing meaningfully with the other. It is surprising, therefore, to find Irmgard Schloegl, in her introduction to the volume, saying of Father Merton's comments that they 'belong to the best that a Westerner has produced' (p. x). This could, of course, be taken as an example of damning with faint praise, especially when one thinks of the worst that Westerners have done in this line. But Dr Schloegl's judgement appears to be made in good faith. Being herself a practical, down to earth kind of person she is, I suspect, over-impressed by the agility with which Father Merton performs on the intellectual tightrope and, with true grandmotherly kindness, concludes that he must have a pair of spiritual wings somewhere that prevent him from falling.

After going through *No Water No Moon* one might be tempted to conclude that hot air rather than wings was the sustaining factor. Whether or not Shree Rajneesh ('Bhagwan' to you!) is 'one of the most highly regarded and admired teachers in India' (back cover blurb) he certainly does have what seems to be increasingly regarded as one of the most indispensable qualifications of a teacher nowadays — the gift of the spiritual gab. Thomas Merton's output of words may have been prodigious but Shree Rajneesh's is spectacular. This is because instead of having the trouble of writing it all out he just talks. In *No Water No Moon* he talks about Zen. Or rather, he talks at length about ten traditional Zen stories, and two admiring female disciples have compiled and edited his comments for our benefit. Let me say at once that Shree Rajneesh talks brilliantly and amusingly — for a few chapters. He also talks excellent sense — on half a dozen pages. Unfortunately, he has the same weakness for intellectual interpretations as Thomas Merton, and really believes that he has explained exactly what each story means. Talking about 'Gutei's Finger', he says, 'Oneness is needed — when the other is not a constant fight. This is why Gutei used to raise one finger whenever he was explaining Zen. He was saying, "Be one! — and all your problems will be solved" '(p. 113). It is interesting to compare this 'explanation' with Yuan Wu's commentary on 'Chu Ti's One Finger Ch'an' in the *Blue Cliff Record*, where the koan on which the story is based originally appeared. 'If you understand at the finger, then you turn your back on Chu Ti; if you don't go to the finger to understand, then it's like cast iron. Whether you understand or not, Chu Ti still goes on this way; whether you're high or low, he still goes on this way; whether you're right or wrong, he still goes on this way' (*The Blue Cliff Record*, pp. 123-124). Shree Rajneesh certainly understands a lot about Zen. In the end we become tired of the constant stream of dogmatic assertions, misleading half truths, and sweeping generalizations — not to mention undigested gobbets of Shree Rajneesh's reading, from the Bible to the Reader's Digest, which are also borne along on the stream. 'Monks are repressed people' (p. 18), 'Rituals are repeated by idiots' (p. 21), 'All temples are inventions of the clever people to exploit the stupid' (p. 4), and 'Enlightened persons are always inconsistent' (p. 143), are good examples of some of his wilder generalizations, and tell us, perhaps, more about himself than about Zen.

Like some other modern teachers, Shree Rajneesh is concerned to invoke the authority of the Buddha, Jesus, etc. for some of his own assertions, and if a suitable quotation is not available he does not hesitate to manufacture one. Thus we learn that 'Buddha never answered questions' (p. 134) and 'Buddha used to say, "Don't ask if you want to be answered. When you don't ask, I will answer. If you ask, the door is closed" (p. 134). Also, Buddha used to insist with newcomers: "For one year remain with me without asking anything. If you ask, you cannot be allowed to live with me, you will have to move. For one year simply be silent" '(p. 134). The purpose of these fabrications — not to use a stronger term — seems to be to make out Bhagavan Buddha to have been very much like 'Bhagwan' Rajneesh, for then 'Bhagwan' Rajneesh would be very much like Bhagavan Buddha. At one point in the talks — given at his Ashram in the fashionable quarter of Poona — Shree Rajneesh even says, 'A Buddha comes — I am here' (p. 128) as though the two were identical. He would do well to take to heart his own excellent advice, 'It is good to sit in a Buddha posture; but remember you are not Buddha' (p. 21).

The back cover blurb tells us, 'This is not the Zen that has been intellectually adopted in the West; it is the Zen of the heart'. I cannot agree. Whatever the Zen that has been adopted in the West may or may not be, there is little doubt that the Zen that has been adopted in these talks resembles mouth Zen rather than heart Zen. Entertaining and instructive though they often are, Shree Rajneesh's thinking is at times so muddled that they will increase rather than decrease the confusion that surrounds the word Zen, and thus in all likelihood do more harm than good. At a time when it has become more necessary than ever to clarify the fundamentals of the spiritual life this is a pity.

The first edition of *The Tiger's Cave* appeared in 1964. Besides talks on the Heart Sutra by Abbot Obora of the

Soto Zen sect (contemporary), these translations of Japanese Zen texts include *Yasenkanna*, an autobiographical narrative by Zen master Hakuin (eighteenth century), and various shorter pieces. In the past thirteen years I have frequently recommended this book, as well as its predecessor *A First Zen Reader*, as one of the very few really good books on Zen, and although many other works on the subject have appeared since it was originally published I find, on reading it again in this new edition, no reason to revise that judgement.

The Wisdom of the Zen Masters*

In the course of the last two or three decades there have been published, in English and other European languages, an enormous number of books on Buddhism, some of them translations of ancient Buddhist texts, others original works, both scholarly and popular, by writers with varying degrees of understanding of the true nature of the Dharma. So great has been the output, indeed, that the Western student is often embarrassed by the riches now placed at his disposal. For such a one, the safest course is for him to confine himself to authentic material which nourishes his own spiritual life and to study that material intensively with a spiritual teacher or, should this be impossible, in the company of like-minded fellow students.

Of the various special forms of Buddhism, few have attracted more attention in recent years than Ch'an or Zen, and though the tide of its popularity now seems to have turned, books on the subject continue to appear. One of the latest of these is *The Wisdom of the Zen Masters*, a collection of stories and sayings with an introduction by the translator, an Austrian Buddhist who spent twelve years in Japan undergoing traditional Zen training, and a foreword by that veteran popularizer of literature on Zen Buddhism, Christmas Humphreys. Among the stories and

The Wisdom of the Zen Masters Translated by Irmgard Schloegl, Foreword by Christmas Humphreys (London: Sheldon Press, 1975)

sayings included are both old favourites like the one about the monk who carried a pretty girl across the river and then put her down on the other side, while his more straightlaced companion continued to carry her in his mind, and ones which to me at least are quite new, like Master Rinzai's 'Do not offer your poem to a man who is not a poet' (p. 55). Though the stories and sayings themselves cover only forty-five pages, Dr Schloegl's harvest is a rich one, and Western Buddhists will find in it much that is both inspiring and instructive, while her introductory essay provides the necessary minimum of background information, as well as several useful reminders, such as that 'Zen is firmly based on the fundamental Buddhist teachings' (p. 3) and that 'There is no specific "body of teaching" in Zen' (p. 38), and some down to earth practical advice. Sticklers for precision of doctrinal statement might however question her seeming identification of the Buddha Nature, or Heart Ground, or Heart, with the 'divinity immanent in creation' of 'Eastern religions' (p. 5).

Quite a number of the stories and sayings, including some of the very best in the collection — such as the three belittling supernatural powers ('supernormal' would have been a better rendering) (pp. 42-43), and my own favourites, the one about the game of chess (p. 61) and the one about Master Kendo, who secretly cooked and ate the scraps which the young monks had wasted (p. 66) are Buddhist rather than specifically Zen, and illustrate the wisdom not so much of Zen Masters as such as of all truly wise and compassionate Buddhists. Indeed, Master Kyogen's statement, 'The painted picture of a dumpling does not take one's hunger away (p. 59) in one form or another is the common property not only of all forms of Buddhism but of all the spiritual traditions of the world. I for one cannot help thinking that, so far as actual practice and experience of the Dharma is concerned at least, it would be better if we spoke in terms of Buddhism rather than in terms of Zen — or, in fact, in terms of any particular school of Buddhism at all.

At the same time, Dr Schloegl's little collection does contain a few anecdotes of the kind which, rightly or wrongly, have come to regarded in the West as typically 'Zen' or 'zennish' — fashionable usages which the author herself deplores (p. 3). Master Takuan, in reply to a question, says that he does not recite the Amida Buddha invocation for fear it might sully his mouth (p. 49). Master Chokhi, asked what is meant by the True Dharma Eye, curtly replies 'Don't just sling dirt about' (p. 59). Master Tanka, to the horror of the temple incumbent, burns a wooden statue of the Buddha for fuel (p. 77). The trouble with anecdotes of this type, of which Dr D. T. Suzuki has given us so many, is that the ordinary Western reader, on the basis of a purely mental understanding of what the Master says or does, tends to identify himself with the enlightened Master of the anecdote rather than with the unenlightened disciple, which encourages the development of a quite unjustified sense of spiritual superiority. Identifying themselves with 'the Master' in this way, some such people have even been known to produce, out of their purely mental understanding, lengthy expositions of Zen, when what they ought to have done was to learn to recite the Amida Buddha invocation, or to cultivate the desire to know what was meant by the True Dharma Eye or the kind of devotion that could be shocked by the destruction of a sacred image. Like their counterparts in the Tibetan tradition, the Zen stories and sayings are essentially *precepts*, that is to say, they are personal teachings directly relating to the individual spiritual needs of the disciple concerned, and should not be read out of context, or taken as applying to people whose spiritual needs may, indeed, be the exact opposite of those of the disciples for whom the teachings were originally meant. Unless this is borne in mind, armchair followers of 'Zen' in the West will continue to regard themselves as having transcended the traditional Buddhist virtues when they have, in fact, yet to develop them. I hope that, despite its small size, Dr Schloegl's attractively produced volume will on the whole tend to discourage aberrations of this kind and help promote the actual practice of the Dharma.

The Gateless Gate*

'We use words to get free from words until we reach the pure wordless Essence.' This quotation from *The Awakening of Faith in the Mahayana* sums up the position of Buddhism with regard to the true function of the various conceptual-cum-verbal formulations which make up what, in the West, is usually referred to as Buddhist philosophy. Far from being an attempt to interrogate the nature of reality by rational means, 'Buddhist Philosophy' is a communication by such means of a reality already experienced, i.e. it is a communication from the enlightened to the unenlightened mind — a communication that makes use of conceptual symbols. In the course of time, however, the conceptual-cum-verbal formulations that made up Buddhist philosophy became so elaborate that their true function was for all practical purposes lost sight of, with the result that in at least some Buddhist circles the study of Buddhist philosophy became, in effect, an end in itself. Thus conceptual symbols came to stand *between* the unenlightened mind and reality. Intellectual understanding of the conceptual-cum-verbal formulations by means of which the enlightened mind communicated its experience of reality was mistaken for the experience — even for the reality — itself. A way had therefore to be

---

* *Gateless Gate* Newly translated with commentary by Zen master Koun Yamada. (Los Angeles: Center Publications, 1979)

found of by-passing conceptual symbols, — of by-passing the intellect, — and communicating the nature of experienced reality by non-conceptual means.

The Ch'an School of China did this mainly with the help of the *kung-an* (Japanese: *koan*). A *kung-an* (literally, 'public document') is the record of a brief encounter between master and disciple, the master's response to the disciple's question being a word or phrase — even an action — that points to ultimate reality without being susceptible to logical interpretation. Collections of koans (the Japanese form has now been naturalized in English, and is therefore to be preferred) were made from the tenth century CE onwards, with verses and comments being added to each koan. Probably the best known and most influential collections are the *Pi Yen Lu* or 'Blue Cliff Record' and the *Mumonkan*, variously translated as 'Gateless Gate' or 'Gateless Barrier'. The latter was compiled and arranged by the 13th century Ch'an master Wu Men (Japanese: Mumon), and consists of forty-eight koans, together with Wu Men's own comments and verses, nearly all of which are quite short. The collection opens with the most famous of all koans, 'Joshu's "Mu!" ' Joshu, (Chinese: Chao-chou), the 9th century Ch'an master, was once asked by a monk, 'Has a dog Buddha nature?' The master replied 'Mu!' ('No', or 'Not'). Practitioners of Ch'an/Zen in China, Japan and, more recently, the West, have been cudgelling their brains about the 'meaning' of this enigmatic reply ever since. Apart from the Buddha Himself, Maitreya, Ananda, Kashyapa, Bodhidharma, and the Sixth Patriarch (Hui Neng), the worthies who appear in the koans are all enlightened Ch'an masters of the period from the 8th to the 12th centuries CE, with most of them being found nearer the beginning than the end of the period. This period, sometimes called the golden age of Ch'an, was the era of the 'latter patriarchs' and their successors, and coincided with the early T'ang Dynasty, the golden age of Chinese civilization.

As one of the outstanding products of the richest and most creative periods of Chinese Ch'an, the *Mumonkan* played an important part in the development of Japanese Zen, being commented on by an uninterrupted series of Zen masters down to the present day. *Gateless Gate* is a new translation of this basic koan collection by Yamada Roshi, a contemporary Japanese Zen master (at least three translations have already appeared in English), together with a collection of *teisho,* or 'commentaries' on the koans, delivered by him to Western practitioners of Zen. The work is not for casual reading. In a sense, it is not for reading at all, and one cannot but admire the attitude of the 12th century Ch'an master who, on finding that Ch'an students had become infatuated with *The Blue Cliff Record,* destroyed the wood blocks of the book and dealt with the koans in a different way. Koans in fact are not material for a good quiet read so much as instruments of meditation — though one does not meditate on them in order to discover their 'meaning'. In other words, their true significance and value emerges only within the context of intensive spiritual practice. The same holds good of the *teisho,* which are not commentaries in the intellectual sense but 'encouragement talks' addressed to actual practitioners of Zen, usually on the occasion of an intensive meditation retreat. Though the work is not for casual reading, studies in a receptive spirit of *Gateless Gate* may however act as a catalyst of spiritual development, and it is for this reason, no doubt, that the book has been made available. Even the casual reader may well be caught unawares! The usefulness of the work is enhanced by a very informative introduction by Thomas Cleary, one of the translators of *The Blue Cliff Record,* as well as by Taizan Maezumi Roshi's foreword, in which we are given very clear explanations of both the koan and the *teisho* as 'basic instructional tools used in traditional Zen training'.

One feels much less happy with the preface by Rev. H. M. Enomiya-Lassalle, S. J., which for some reason or other it has been thought necessary to add to all the other preliminary matter. It contains some very questionable statements. According to this Jesuit admirer of Zen, 'Christians have found and are continuing to find that they can attempt Yoga and Zen without jeopardizing their own religion' (p. xiii). When the practice of Zen jeopardizes Buddhism itself, one wonders what sort of Zen the Christians referred to could have 'attempted' if it leaves their own religion intact. (Perhaps there is an ambiguity in the use of the word religion here.) In the same ecumenical spirit, Father Enomiya-Lassalle also tells us that 'the end, whether called "God" or "Absolute" is after all ONE'. What would he make of a koan that does not appear in the *Mumonkan*, which asks, 'If all things are reduced to the One, to what will you reduce the One'? Perhaps his most questionable statement is that 'Zen practice has nothing to do with Buddhist philosophy'. If by this he means that Zen does not regard Buddhist philosophy as an end in itself he is giving expression to a truism. If on the other hand he means (as he appears to mean) that Zen has no more to do with Buddhist philosophy — and presumably no more to do with Buddhism — than with the philosophy of Aristotle or St Thomas Aquinas his statement is both false and misleading. What it does, in effect, is to reduce Patriarchal Ch'an to Tathagata Ch'an, i.e. it reduces the practice of Zen to a matter of concentration and concentration techniques, which of course do not, in themselves, jeopardize any religion, and can be combined with any philosophy. By reducing Zen in this way liberal Catholic thinkers like Father Enomiya-Lassalle hope to 'contain' Zen and thus neutralize its influence. That they should want to do this is not surprising. What is surprising is that a Buddhist organization like the Zen Center of Los Angeles should appear to countenance the attempt.

The Wisdom of Tibet*

Speaking in terms of cultural geography, there are at present three major historical forms of Buddhism extant in the world. These are South-east Asian Buddhism, which is found in Sri Lanka, Burma, and Thailand, as well as in Cambodia and Laos; Sino-Japanese Buddhism, which exists not only in China and Japan but also in Korea and Vietnam; and Tibetan Buddhism, which from the Land of Snows spreads into Mongolia, Sikkim, Bhutan, and Ladhak. In terms of the three yanas South-east Asian Buddhism belongs to the Hinayana. Sino-Japanese Buddhism to the combined Hinayana and Mahayana, with the latter predominating, especially in Japan, while Tibetan Buddhism belongs equally to the Hinayana, the Mahayana, and the Vajrayana, with each succeeding yana providing the orientation for the preceding one. As for the specific traditions by which they are represented, South-East Asian Buddhism is represented by the Theravada,

*Tenzin Gyatso, the Fourth Dalai Lama *The Buddhism of Tibet and the Key to the Middle Way* Translated in the main by Jeffrey Hopkins and Lati Rimpoche (London: George Allen & Unwin, 1975)

Nagarjuna and the Seventh Dalai Lama, *The Precious Garland and The Song of The Four Mindfulnesses* Translated and edited by Jeffrey Hopkins and Lati Rimpoche with Anne Klein. Foreword by His Holiness Tenzin Gyatso, the Fourteenth Dalai Lama. (London: George Allen & Unwin, 1975)

Mind in Buddhist Psychology Translated from the Tibetan by Herbert V. Guenther and Leslie Kawamura (Dharma Publishing, 1975)

Sino-Japanese Buddhism on the practical side mainly by Chan/Zen and Chin T'u/Shin and on the theoretical side by the T'ien T'ai and Hua Yen (Avatamsaka) schools, and Tibetan Buddhism by the Nyingmapa, Kagyupa, Sakyapa, and Gelugpa schools.

All three forms of Buddhism are continuations of Indian Buddhism as it existed at a certain historical stage of its development. This is particularly true of Tibetan Buddhism. Though elements from Central Asia may have enriched the final synthesis, and though outstanding Tibetan Buddhist personalities like Milarepa and Tsongkhapa undoubtedly made original contributions of great value, Tibetan Buddhism is essentially the brilliant and complex Buddhism of the Pala Dynasty in North-eastern India transported as it were bodily from the sub-tropical plains and forests of Bengal and Bihar across the mighty barrier of the Himalayas into the icy, windswept table-lands of Tibet. This transportation was not like the transferal of an artefact from one place to another, but rather resembled the translation of living bodies which, while continuing faithfully to transmit their ancestral lineaments, at the same time adapted themselves to their new environment and propogated there a strong and vigorous new generation of their kind. In matters of monastic organization and general doctrinal teaching Tibetan Buddhism perpetuates the Sarvastivada. In 'Philosophy' it is the true successor of the twin schools of the Madhyamika and the Yogachara, the 'profound' and the 'sublime'. As regards Tantric spiritual practice, it keeps alive the symbolic rituals and esoteric meditations of a hundred different lineages of Indian yogis and adepts.

Now the old Tibet is gone, and some of its most distinguished representatives are scattered to the four corners of the earth. The loss, appalling though it is, has been compensated for to a small extent by the increase of interest in Tibetan Buddhism which has occurred in many parts of Western Europe and the North American continent — an interest which, so far as the English language at least is concerned, finds both expression and powerful reinforcement in an ever-growing body of new books on Tibetan Buddhism. With the appearance of these publications, which include translations of classics of Tibetan Buddhist literature as well as works of modern Western scholarship, the true nature of Tibetan Buddhism is gradually becoming better known — so far as it can be known in this way.

Some of these new publications, like the first two volumes of the Wisdom of Tibet Series, 'Published under the aegis of the Library of Tibetan Works and Archives with the authority of His Holiness the Dalai Lama as revealing oral tradition', bear witness to the fidelity with which the Buddhists of Tibet have preserved the teachings committed to them by their Indian masters. The first volume of the series, *The Buddhism of Tibet and the Key to the Middle Way*, is by the Dalai Lama himself, and as the title indicates consists of two separate works. The first of these is a revised version of the appendix called *An Outline of Buddhism in Tibet* in the Dalai Lama's book of memoirs *My Land and My People*. It consists of a series of short sections on such fundamental topics as the Four Noble Truths, Liberation, Hinayana, Mahayana, Tantrayana, the Two Truths, Training in Higher Meditative Stabilization, and the Mind of Enlightenment. As one would have expected, the Dalai Lama's approach to his subject is 'orthodox' in the true sense of the term, being firmly based on traditional sources, both literal and oral. No concessions are made to contemporary *mithyādrishtis*, however fashionable. Barring the occasional obscurity due to extreme conciseness of expression, the exposition is very clear, and it is evident to how great an extent Tibetan Buddhism coincides with the two other major cultural-geographical expressions of the Dharma. The second work in the volume is more advanced. In it the Dalai Lama — who won his degree as a geshe or 'Doctor of Buddhist Philosophy' the hard way after years of study with the best teachers and a gruelling public *vive voce* — gives a resume of the doctrine of the Middle Way as expounded by the great teachers of the Prasangika-Madhyamika school. According to this school, the Middle Way is much more than a golden mean between the extremes of hedonistic self-indulgence and ascetic self-mortification. Its significance is essentially 'metaphysical', consisting in the fact that dependently-arising phenomena abide in a 'middle way', being neither truly and inherently existent nor utterly non-existent, and that this 'middle wayness' of phenomena is identical with their voidness and emptiness. Voidness and emptiness is the object of true cognition, which is not the cognition of the non-existence *in* phenomena of an existent object, not even of an object called 'emptiness', but simply the cognition of the absence in phenomena of their own inherent existence. Such cognition is also cognition of the non-existence, in the ultimate sense, of the 'I-ness' which is the basis for the arising of craving, hatred, and so on. For this reason it is of the greatest practical importance. It is the cognition of emptiness which makes the difference between worldly life and spiritual life, suffering and happiness, bondage and liberation, and on this point the Dalai Lama insists with great earnestness.

Like the classic Indian treatises on which it is based, and from which it profusely quotes, *The Key to the Middle Way* approaches its great subject in a way that, despite the unfortunate devaluation that the word has undergone in recent years, can only be described as 'intellectual', and its method of treatment is scholastic. At intervals, an imaginary opponent raises objections, which are conscientiously shown to be without foundation. We are reminded of Aquinas rather than of Schopenhauer or Nietzsche. Indeed, the Dalai Lama has a faith in reason, and a willingness to use it to the limit of its capacity, which nowadays is not often encountered in 'religious' circles, least of all in those devoted to 'The Wisdom of the East'. Commenting on the last of Maitreya's 'four reliances', he says, 'With respect to a non-conceptual wisdom that apprehends a profound emptiness, one first cultivates a conceptual consciousness that apprehends the emptiness, and when a clear perception of the object of meditation arises, this becomes a non-conceptual wisdom. *Moreover, the initial generation of that conceptual consciousness must depend solely on a correct reasoning'* (pp. 55-56. My italics). Even when speaking, in the first work in the volume, of the special meditation practices of the Highest Yoga (Anuttara-Yoga) of the Tantrayana, he is careful to add, 'Although there are definitely instances of achievements among these paths through the power of belief, these powers are mostly achieved through the power of reasoning' (p. 30). To those for whom Tibetan Buddhism is all magic and mystery, who see it through a thick haze of pseudo-occult 'romance', or a fog of sentiment, the sunlit rationality of the Dalai Lama's approach may well come as a shock.

The second volume in the Wisdom of Tibet Series also contains two works, the second of which is a translation of the Tibetan version of the *Ratnamālā* (otherwise known as the *Ratnāvalī*) or 'Precious Garland' of Nagarjuna — the second and/or third century 'popularizer' of the Perfection of Wisdom sutras, inaugurator of the Madhyamika tradition, and perhaps the greatest name in Indian Mahayana Buddhism. Not that we are, in reality, as far removed from the original text as we might think. Sanskrit

Buddhist manuscripts, where they exist at all, are very corrupt, and Tibetan translations are very faithful. An English version of the Tibetan translation, made with the help of a Tibetan teacher 'in the lineage', may well get us closer to the original Indian author's real meaning than would a translation made from the actual Sanskrit text by a Western scholar who had no access to the oral explanations of the text which are — or were — transmitted in Tibet as part of the total tradition. The work is addressed to an unnamed king, supposedly one belonging to the South Indian Śātavāhana dynasty, and consists of five chapters each containing one hundred verses. Two of the chapters are here translated for the first time, the remaining three having been translated by G. Tucci and published in 1934-36. In Chapter 1, 'High Status and Definite Goodness', a short account of the practices conducive to high status, i.e. rebirth in a state of happiness as a man or god, is followed by a longer and more detailed description of the wisdom by means of which one achieves definite goodness, i.e. liberation and omniscience. For Nagarjuna, of course, this wisdom is the cognition of the emptiness expounded by the Buddha in the Perfection of Wisdom sutras. Chapter 2 is 'An Interwoven Explanation of Definite Goodness and High Status' and includes, among other teachings, a further explanation of the truth of emptiness, an exhortation to reflect on the foulness of a woman's body as an antidote to lust, and a description of the particular virtuous deeds which lead to the acquisition of each of the thirty-two major marks of a Buddha. Chapter 3 is devoted to 'The Collections for Enlightenment', the collections being, of course, those of merit and wisdom. (For some reason the translators fail to distinguish between prajñā/sherab and jñāna/yeshe, rendering both as 'wisdom'.) Among other things, the king is advised to provide for the propogation of the Dharma, to maintain a wide variety of social services, to provide food for ants, and to eliminate high taxes. Chapter 4 is entitled 'Royal Policy' and contains Nagarjuna's advice to the king as king. After exhorting him to govern not only with justice but with compassion (prisoners are to be made comfortable so long as they are not freed, while murderers are simply to be banished), he urges him to renounce attachment to the senses, which in any case are not truly real. This leads to another discussion of wisdom, which by way of a reference to the merits and wisdom of the Bodhisattva in turn leads to a vigorous defence of the Mahayana as the veritable word of the Buddha. Interestingly enough, Nagarjuna makes no criticism of the Hinayana, clearly regarding the two teachings as being in essence identical. The Mahayana is the fuller explanation of what is taught in brief in the Hinayana — particularly as regards the actual practice of the Bodhisattva Ideal. Despite the excellence of the advice he has given him, Nagarjuna realizes that it might be hard for him to rule religiously in an unrighteous world. In that case, the right thing for the king to do is to become a monk. Chapter 5, 'Bodhisattva Deeds', describes the various practices in which he should then engage. First, there are more than fifty-seven faults to be given up, after which the perfections are to be cultivated. These are briefly described, as are the ten stages of a Bodhisattva's progress and their fruits. In order to develop his faith in the limitlessness of the Buddha's qualities the king is advised to recite twenty stanzas three times a day in front of an image or reliquary. These twenty stanzas are a version of the Sevenfold Puja, with a particularly extensive Rejoicing in Merits. As the translators observe in their introduction, the *Precious Garland of Advice to the King (Rājaparikathā-ratnamālā)*, to give it its full title, is renowned among the works of Nagarjuna for its comprehensive description of the two inseparable aspects of the Bodhisattva's life, his realization, through wisdom, of the profound emptiness, and his fulfilment, through compassion, of the extensive deeds. The *Ratnamālā* is thus a *veda mecum* of the Mahayana from both the 'theoretical' and the practical points of view, and as such it has ever been highly esteemed by Tibetan Buddhists. As such, I hope, it will come to be esteemed by Western Buddhists too. Its inclusion in the present volume makes available to us in full one of the masterpieces of Indian Mahayana expository literature — succinct, comprehensive, and inspiring. It also enables us to appreciate the kind of material that has been preserved by the lamas of Tibet, and that contributed to the creation of that many-splendoured thing known to us in the West as Tibetan Buddhism. The remaining work in the volume is entitled *Instructions for Meditation on the View of Emptiness, The Song of the Four Mindfulnesses, Causing the Rain of Achievements to Fall,* by the Seventh Dalai Lama (1708-1757 CE). Though very much shorter than the *Ratnamālā,* being only two pages long, its spiritual value is no less. The Four Mindfulnesses are not those which are included in the Thirty-Seven helps to Enlightenment, but a special Tantric set, consisting of Mindfulness of the Teacher, of the Altruistic Aspiration to the Highest Enlightenment (Bodhichitta), of Your Body as a Divine Body, and of the View of Emptiness. The inclusion of this little work, based on a personal revelation to Tsongkhapa by the Bodhisattva Manjushri, illustrates the importance of the Tantrayana in the spiritual life of Tibet, besides providing us with a fine example of an original Tibetan contribution to Buddhist literature. The extreme shortness of the work can be taken, perhaps, as hinting at the fact that specifically Tantric teachings cannot be made available so easily, or indeed in the same way, as those of the two other yanas.

One of the most important developments of Indian Buddhism to be introduced into Tibet was the Abhidharma. For five hundred years, from the time of Ashoka to the time of Nagarjuna, it dominated the field to such an extent that it has recently been suggested that this period, generally known as the Hinayana period, should be called instead the Age of Abhidharma. Even at the time of the introduction of Buddhism into Tibet, from the 7th to the 12th century CE, it was still influential. Basically, the Abhidharma was an attempt to clarify and systematize the Buddha's teachings as contained in the sutras. As such it may be described as a form of scholasticism, though with the proviso that it is concerned not so much with metaphysics as with psychology. There were three distinct, though not dissimilar, Abhidharma traditions: those of the Sarvastivada, the Theravada, and the Yogachara. Only the first and third of these were introduced into Tibet. *Mind in Buddhist Psychology* is a translation of 'The Necklace of Clear Understanding: An Elucidation of the Working of Mind and Mental Events' by Ye-shes gyal-tsham, an eighteenth century Tibetan lama of the Gelugpa school, and the work represents a continuation, on Tibetan soil, of the Indian Yogachara Abhidharma tradition. In form it is an auto-commentary of the author's own verse text, which explains the mind and its fifty-one mental events in 177 four-lined stanzas. As the translators point out, Ye-shes gyal-tsham's presentation of his subject is closely modelled on the *Abhidharma-samuccaya* or 'Compendium of Abhidharma' of Asanga, the originator on earth of the Yogachara tradition, helped out by plentiful quotations from the *Lam-rim chen-mo* or 'Great Stages of the Path' by Tsongkhapa, the founder of the Gelugpa school. Not counting the Verses of Veneration and Intention, with which it opens, the work falls into five sections, the third of which deals with 'Mind' and the fourth with 'Mental

Events'. The author's purpose in discussing the subject is, of course, strictly practical. We all experience frustration. This frustration has a cause, which is the power of karma and the emotions, i.e. our own mind. Moreover, it is the mind, the positive mind, that gives rise to all spiritual qualities and attainments. Mind is the root of both *saṁsāra* and Nirvana. Consequently, it is essential to know what is meant by mind and mental events, and to be able to distinguish positive mental events from negative ones, so that the former can be cultivated and the latter rejected. For Ye-shes gyal-tsham, as for the Abhidharma tradition generally, psychological analysis is undertaken not as an end in itself but for the sake of gaining from it an understanding that can be transformed into a living experience — an experience that culminates in Enlightenment.

Following his Indian authorities, the author defines mind as the awareness of the factual presence of a particular object, and mental events as the becoming involved with this object by way of other specific functions. Between mind as the primary factor and the mental events as its 'entourage' there exist five functional co-relations, of which two partly differing accounts are given, one deriving from the Sarvastivada, the other from the Yogachara. Mental events are said to be altogether fifty-one in number. Five are omnipresent, i.e. operate in the wake of every mind situation; five are object-determining; eleven are of a positive nature; six are basic emotions, and are of a negative nature; twenty are proximate emotions and also negative; and four are variables, being so called because they become positive, or negative, or indeterminate, according to the level and quality of the mental situation. All these mental events are described in detail, with the result that this section of 'The Necklace of Clear Understanding' is not only the longest but also the most interesting and useful of the whole work. We find, for instance, that what Guenther terms 'directionality of mind (*sems-pa*), one of the five omnipresent mental events, is the most important of all mental events whatever. It is what propels forward the mind and its corresponding mental events and causes them to settle on an object. We also find that faith (or confidence, as the translators prefer to call it) comes first in the list of eleven positive mental events which are essential to spiritual development, and that it is described as consisting of a *lucid faith* that realizes the value of The Three Jewels, a *trusting faith* that sees the connection between one's action and its consequences, and a *longing faith* that moves one to aspire to the realization of the Four Noble Truths by one's own efforts' (p. 39). Though in his discussion of the different kinds of mental events Ye-shes gyal-tsham relies on the *Abhidharma-Samuccaya* and the *Lam-rim chen-mo*, he does at the same time have something original to contribute. Indeed, we are throughout very much aware of the venerable author's presence as, with great kindliness and patience, and with deep feeling for his subject, he guides us through the complexities of what may be considered the central theme of the Abhidharma. What a wonderful teacher he must have been! Even in the old Tibet, however, things were not always as they should have been. Ye-shes gyal-tsham has to lament that 'Those who realize the works of the Sages and sublime persons of India as the very foundation of instructions are like the stars in daytime' (p. 40) and that, in words that have a familiar ring, 'young people nowadays do not consider this division between good and evil as very important' (p. 62). Probably the truth of the matter is that, however favourable outward conditions may be, there will always be some who do not care to devote themselves to the study of the Dharma. Similarly, however unfavourable such conditions may be, some will always be found who, for the sake of obtaining the gift of the Dharma, are prepared to undergo any hardship, to make any sacrifice. At the present day, even in the West, there are many who will welcome such a book as *Mind in Buddhist Psychology*. Though writers on Buddhism often sing the praises of Buddhist psychology, telling us how profound it is, and how far in advance of its modern Western counterparts, we are very rarely given any concrete information about it. One of the merits of the present work is that it consists of nothing but concrete information, clearly and systematically presented. Indeed, it is the best traditional exposition of the mysteries of the Abhidharma available to the English-speaking Western reader — the best modern exposition is Dr Guenther's *Philosophy and Psychology in the Abhidharma* (1956) — and I recommend it as highly suitable for adoption as a text book for study courses in the Abhidharma. The work would have been still more useful if the translators had given us the original Sanskrit of the numerous psychological terms, as well as their Tibetan equivalents. Perhaps they would argue that in the course of centuries the Tibetan equivalents acquired subtle connotations of their own, but even so it seems strange that the Sanskrit terms should not be given even in the numerous quotations from Indian works — more especially as the work is liberally peppered with Dr Guenther's highly individual, not to say idiosyncratic, renderings of standard Buddhist terms. Thus, in the absence of the Sanskrit, how is the uninformed reader to know that 'inspection' corresponds to 'mindfulness', or that 'analytical-appreciative understanding', which is Dr Guenther's translation of prajñā/sherab, corresponds to what less brilliant scholars uniformly render as 'wisdom'? Perhaps Dr Guenther wants his writings and translations to constitute a self-contained world of their own, without signposts to other worlds. If so, it is a pity, for it is a world well worth exploring. It also seems strange that, whereas the names of the two translators appear on the title page, the name of the author does not. *Pūjā ca pūjanīyānaṁ*. No doubt the omission, which must have been due to an oversight, will be rectified in a further edition, which I hope will soon be called for.

The Religions of Tibet and Mongolia*

Every year the number of books on Buddhism published in English is increasing, and more and more of them are showing signs of a deeper understanding of the Dharma than was often the case even twenty years ago. It is no longer a question of having to distinguish the partly reliable from the totally unreliable so much as a question of having to distinguish the partly unreliable from the almost totally reliable. It is also a question — so far as the FWBO is concerned — of having to distinguish what is relevant to the needs of the Buddhist Spiritual Community in twentieth century England, New Zealand, Finland, and India (to begin with) from what is not relevant to those needs. Many of the books now appearing are of sufficient importance to demand full length review articles. All that can be offered, on the present occasion, is short notices of

---

*Giuseppe Tucci *The Religions of Tibet* Translated from the German and Italian by Geoffrey Samuel (London & Henley: Routledge & Kegan Paul, 1980)

The Life and Teaching of Geshe Rabten: A Tibetan Lama's Search for Truth Translated and edited by B. Alan Wallace (Gelong Jhampa Kelsang),(London: George Allen & Unwin)

Walther Heissig *The Religions of Mongolia* Translated from the German edition by Geoffrey Samuel (London & Henley: Routledge & Kegan Paul)

a random but not unrepresentative selection of the books already received for review this year.

According to the publishers, Giuseppe Tucci's *The Religions of Tibet* is the first comprehensive account of Tibetan Buddhism to be published in English since Waddell's *Buddhism of Tibet* appeared in 1894. This does not take into account Hoffmann's *The Religions of Tibet* (1961), but there is no doubt that this rich and readable book by 'one of the greatest scholars whom Buddhist studies has so far produced' (E. Conze) is far and away the best 'overview of the Tibetan Buddhist world' (p. ix) that we have yet been given. Despite its comprehensiveness, it is no mere historical survey of religious developments *ab extra* but a sensitive exploration of the depths of the Tibetan religious spirit. After summarizing the diffusion of Buddhism in Tibet in two admirably concise chapters, Professor Tucci plunges into the heart of his subject with three masterly chapters on the general characteristics of Lamaism, the doctrines of the most important schools, and monkhood, monastery life, the religious calendar, and festivals. These chapters, which form the central part of the book, probably bring us closer to the real nature of Tibetan Buddhism than all the previous lucubrations on the subject put together. There are also chapters on the folk religion of Tibet and the *Bon* religion. Throughout the book Professor Tucci draws on an extensive knowledge of Tibetan texts, as well as on personal observation and research in Western and Central Tibet. In order to illustrate a point, he is even able to refer to his own experience when he obtained the consecration of *Kye rdo rje* in *Sa skya* (p. 82). Yet great as his learning is he is never overwhelmed by it. At every turn we are impressed by his easy mastery of his complex material, his capacity for lucid exposition and his great power of expression. Whether expounding the views of the different Buddhist schools on the nature of the relation between light and mind (*'od gsel* and *sems*), describing the economic structure of the monasteries, or explaining the origins of the New Year's Festival, he is invariably well informed, penetrating and judicious.

With much of the book representing the results of previously unpublished research, a number of things not clear before are clarified, while things that were already clear receive further clarification. We are made aware of the extent to which political motives were involved in the introduction of Buddhism into Tibet (p. 6), as well as of the fact that the monastic communities were institutions of economic power, and therefore decisive factors in Tibetan history (p. 25). Indeed, we are told that the secular power of the religious communities released 'a militant attitude which aspired to hegemony in the temporal world as well as in the spiritual' (p. 27). Emphasis is laid on the experience of pure, undifferentiated light as the common fundamental trait of the entire course of the religious experience of Tibetan man, and on the fact that 'the magical and gnostic foundations of Tantrism lend their unmistakable imprint to the whole Lamaist way of thinking and practice' (p. 93). In connection with this latter point Professor Tucci finds it necessary to stress the importance of soteriological goals for Tibetan Buddhism. 'It would be a great error, and reveal an insufficient understanding of the special nature of Tibetan Buddhism,' he says, perhaps with some of his more 'academic' colleagues in mind, 'if one were to disregard the soteriological goals permeating and dominating it. It is not a question here of a purely intellectual process, not of the acquisition of theoretical knowledge, but rather of the alignment of the entire cognitive activity towards the goal of salvation. All along the line intellectual understanding remains subordinate to lived experience' (p. 93). This could hardly be better expressed. Soteriological goals may, however, be obscured by the magical and exorcistic preoccupations of the folk religion. In speaking of the 'particular psychic disposition of the Tibetan' Professor Tucci more than once reminds us that the Tibetan 'lives in a permanent state of anxious uneasiness' (pp. 172-173), and that 'the entire spiritual life of the Tibetan is defined by a permanent attitude of defence, by a constant effort to appease and propitiate the powers whom he fears' (p. 187). He also draws attention to the fact that a remarkable characteristic of Tibetan religiosity is 'its striking lack of social compassion' (p. 210). Though the Bodhisattva vow is recited daily, 'the teachings enshrined in the vow rarely receive more than a vague theoretical assertion' (p. 211).

One of the most interesting features of Professor Tucci's book is the way in which he regularly describes the Buddhism of Tibet as 'Lamaism'. For most scholars this term, first apparently used by Köpen (1859), and presumably coined by him, is now obsolete. As long ago as 1914 Waddell himself, writing in Hastings' *Encyclopaedia of Religion and Ethics* (Vol. 7, p. 784), characterized it as 'in many ways misleading, inappropriate, and undesirable', adding that it was 'rightly dropping out of use'. Rightly or wrongly, Professor Tucci has now revived the term. This is not so surprising as it might seem. One of the facts which emerges most strongly from his whole 'overview' is the extent to which Tibetan Buddhism is the product of creative interaction between Indian Buddhism on the one hand and, on the other, the 'pre-Buddhist beliefs, myths, rituals, and invocatory formulae of Tibet' (p. 30). For so distinctive a synthesis a distinctive term is needed, and it may well be that the old term Lamaism is the most appropriate. The use of such a term is not without its advantages for Western Buddhists. It reminds us that Tibetan Buddhism is quite as much Tibetan as Buddhist, and that inasmuch as it is, in part, the product of a culture very different from our own, there can be no question of the whole system being transported bodily from Tibet to the West.

In *The Religions of Tibet* the life of the monastic communities is one subject among many, and we hear about it from a sympathetic observer. In *The Life and Teachings of Geshe Rabten* it is virtually the only subject, and we hear about it from one who, for more than twenty years, experienced it for himself. Though he tells us little that we cannot learn from Professor Tucci (the Professor, indeed, tells us much that we do not learn from the Geshe), he gives us an incomparably more vivid and fascinating picture of daily life in a great Tibetan monastic establishment than we could possibly obtain from any second hand account, however informative. Born in Kham (Eastern Tibet) in 1920(?), of farming stock, the young Tadin Rabten grew up more familiar with horses, dogs, and guns, than with books. When he was fifteen he noticed how 'simple, pure, and efficient' the lives of the monks were, and at seventeen decided to join one of the monastic universities. Two years later, having made the three month journey to Lhasa, he was admitted to Sera Monastery, the second largest in Tibet. From then onwards his days — and sometimes his nights as well — were devoted to study and religious practices. Only in 1959, at the time of the Lhasa uprising, was he affected by the presence of the Chinese. By that time he had decided to take the Geshe examination, which he eventually passed in India, as a refugee, after twenty-four years of hard work. In order to qualify he had to pass through fifteen classes, familiarizing himself with such subjects as Logic and Epistemology, Abhidharma, Vinaya, the Perfection of Wisdom, and Madhyamika. The first subject he was taught, however, was the relationship between the four primary and eight secondary colours. Besides engaging in doctrinal studies he memorized thousands of pages of texts, participated in endless formal debates, practised meditation, recited prayers and mantras, and rose before dawn to perform prostrations. Such was his zeal that he was content with a minimum of food and clothing, often going hungry for days on end and wearing nothing but rags held together with bits of wire. Not surprisingly, when he visited his old home after six years of monastic life he found that his outlook had changed. 'Even when I looked up at the pastures where I had loved to roam as a child, I felt no attraction. The same was true of my home. Nothing interested me. It was all rather depressing. I found that my way of thinking had changed entirely' (p. 74).

Despite the hardships, life at Sera Monastery suited Geshe Rabten very well. Study and meditation brought their own rewards, while the kindness with which the monks treated one another — older monks making personal sacrifices in order to assist younger monks and newcomers — helped to create an atmosphere of warmth and spiritual friendship. His strongest emotional ties were with his teachers, for whom he felt boundless reverence and devotion — a devotion that finds heartfelt utterance in a letter written to his principal guru, Geshe Jhampa Khedup, which appears in the first part of the book, containing the story of his life. Devotion is, in fact, the keynote of Geshe Rabten's character. Combined with deep understanding, and wide learning, it is very much in evidence not only in the first, but also in the second part of the book, containing his teachings. In this part the Geshe deals mainly with the 'three principles of the path', i.e. with renunciation, 'an awakening mind' (i.e. the bodhichitta), and the ideal view. He also gives us an Introduction to the Buddhadharma, an explanation of the (Tantric) Preliminary Practices, and instruction in 'mental quiescence' (i.e. *śamatā*). Reading these clear and practical teachings, one cannot but conclude that they represent the noble fruit of a noble life.

Such is the nobility and disinterestedness of Geshe Rabten's life, indeed, that one is reluctant to make even the smallest criticism of the system that produced him. Criticism based on modern, secular notions of education would be irrelevant in any case. As the Geshe himself points out, a monastic university like Sera differs from a Western university in that only the Buddhadharma is studied, and in that because the field of training is the Dharma, the mind experiences greater and greater happiness, regardless of physical hardships. Nonetheless it must be said that, reading the story of Geshe Rabten's life, one gets the impression that under the Gelugpa system of monastic training there was a distinct overemphasis on doctrinal and scholastic studies. The Gelugpa system in fact seems to have favoured intellectual *cramming*, It is not without significance, perhaps, that Geshe Rabten more than once has recourse to the image of the factory. Speaking of his early years at Sera, for example, he says, 'Many people working in a factory have nothing to occupy their attention but their daily routine. Similarly in the monastery throughout the day and night, I had nothing to think of but the Dharma' (p. 53). Some Western Buddhists might find the idea of a monastery being a *factory* less than appealing. They might wonder whether it was *really* the function of a monastery to produce geshes — even geshes as devout and learned as Geshe Rabten. They might even wonder whether an exhaustive study of all the different schools of 'Buddhist philosophy' was *really* necessary to the attainment of Enlightenment. Considerations of this sort become all the more pressing when, towards the end of his career, we find Geshe Rabten receiving from six to ten 'empowerments' (i.e. *abhiṣekas*, or 'consecrations' as Tucci calls them) every day for weeks on end. Significantly, he says of the daily recitations of the corresponding rituals that they never took so much time that his studies were impaired (p. 111). It would seem that much as Geshe Rabten gained for his twenty-four years of intensive study, something was also lost.

Both geographically and culturally, the step from Tibet to Mongolia is not a very great one. Walter Heissig's *The Religions of Mongolia* is the companion volume to Guiseppe Tucci's *The Religions of Tibet*, the two having been first published together in German as parts of a single work. It is, however, a very different kind of book. Not only is it much shorter, but it devotes far more space to the shamanistic folk religion of the Mongols than it does to Mongolian Buddhism. There are two reasons for this. In the first place, judging by the twenty-nine items listed under his name in the bibliography, Professor Heissig is more interested in Mongolian shamanism than in Mongolian Buddhism, having personally collected from the libraries of Europe seventy-eight manuscripts containing prayers, invocations, and so on. The part of the book dealing with the non-Buddhist folk religion of the Mongols is in fact firmly based on original sources. In the second place, 'the forms of Northern Buddhism in Mongolia correspond to those of Tibet from which they originated' (p. ix), and there was no point in Professor Heissig describing what Professor Tucci had already described. 'Although numerous Mongolian lamas made substantial contributions to Lamaist theology [sic], which were significantly all composed in Tibetan, the church [sic] language of Lamaism, the Mongolian theological schools, developed no divergent doctrinal interpretations. Only in those cases where . . . the Mongolian folk religion was incorporated in a syncretic fashion into the doctrinal edifice of Lamaism, did there take place any truly local development' (p. 34). This about sums up the matter. Professor Heissig is therefore left free to concentrate on the 'beliefs and concepts which belong to the non-Buddhist folk religion of the Mongols' (p. ix), such as those relating to the mythical Cinggis Khan, the deity of fire, and the 'White Old Man', giving us only a short description of the spread of Lamaism in Mongolia, though there are also chapters on the relation between Lamaism and the folk religion and the Lamaist suppression of shamanism. (In case anyone should raise the cry of 'intolerance' against Buddhism on this account, let it be noted that the suppression consisted in the abolition of human and animal sacrifice and the burning of the felt Ongghot dolls.)

Even the short description that Professor Heissig gives us of the spread of Lamaism in Mongolia is not without significance for Western Buddhists. As with the dissemination of Buddhism in Tibet, political as well as spiritual factors played an important part. Chinese emperors favoured the spread of Lamaism into Mongolia from China, where it had flourished since the Yuan dynasty, mainly as a means of pacifying the warlike Mongols, while Mongol princes saw in it a means of boosting their political prestige. 'Conversion' tended to take place 'from above'. In 1578, on the occasion of his first meeting with the Third Dalai Lama, Altan Khan had a number of noblemen, princes among them, 'enter the priestly state |sic|' (p. 29). As Professor Heissig observes, 'It is difficult to avoid the impression that part of the conversion consisted in acts of the government' (p. 29). Earlier on, there were the usual misunderstandings about 'Tantrism', i.e. the Vajrayana. Tantric ritual was understood as a more efficacious form of worldly magic than shamanism, while Tantric sexual symbolism was taken quite literally, with disastrous results. Eventually, Lamaism was established throughout Mongolia, retaining its influence until the middle of the twentieth century. According to Professor Heissig, the downfall began with the decay of Manchu power, and when 'the divergence between preaching and reality |on the part of the monks| was no longer to be bridged' (p. 35).

Padmasambhava Comes to the West*

With his lotus cap, his red cloak, and trident resting in the crook of his left arm, the figure of Padmasambhava is one of the most striking and distinctive in the whole range of Buddhism. Well do I remember the tremendous impression it made upon me when, in the early 'fifties, I encountered it for the first time in the gloom of a temple in the foothills of the Eastern Himalayas. In English very little information about Guru Rimpoche, or the Precious Master, as the Tibetans generally call Padmasambhava, has been available. We had 'An Epitome of the Life and Teachings of Tibet's great *guru* Padmasambhava' in Evans-Wentz's *The Tibetan Book of the Great Liberation* (1954), and a chapter on Padmasambhava and Padmaiem (sic) in Hoffman's *The Religions of Tibet* (1961), as well as various short summaries of his career in books about Tibet and histories of Buddhism, and that was about all. Now under the title of *The Life and Liberation of Padmasambhava*, Tarthang Tulku has brought out, in two bulky volumes, an English version of the French translation of the *Padma bKa'i Thang*, so that at last we are able to follow in detail the

The Life and Liberation of Padmasambhava (Padma bKa'i Thang) As Recorded by Yeshe Tsogyal, Rediscovered by Terchen Urgyan Lingpa, Translated into French as *Le Dict de Padma* by Gustave-Charles Toussaint, Translated into English by Kenneth Douglas and Gwendolyn Bays, Corrected with the Original Tibetan Manuscripts and with an Introduction by Tarthang Tulku (Emeryville, California: Dharma Publishing, 1978)

career of the extraordinary being who was mainly responsible for introducing Buddhism into Tibet and whose magical personality has dominated the spiritual lives, and fired the imaginations, of a large section of the Tibetan people ever since.

The *Padma bKa'i Thang* is a terma or 'treasure' text which we are told was taken from the heart of the fierce deity guarding the door of the Crystal Rock Cave by Urgyan Lingpa, its preordained revealer, in 1326, after it had lain concealed within the image for more than five centuries. The original authorship of the text is attributed to Yeshe Tsogyal, one of the twenty-five principal disciples of Padmasambhava. The work is divided into 108 Cantos, as the English translator calls them, the first fifty-three of which have been assigned to Part 1 of this edition under the heading 'India' and the remaining fifty-five to Part 2 under 'Tibet'. According to the English translator's preface, 'In many respects this work in two volumes is comparable to the Germanic sagas or the Greek and Roman epics' (p. xx). So far as the Greek and Roman epics are concerned, the comparison is not really valid. Though the story line is reasonably clear and continuous the *Padma bKa'i Thang* is a somewhat chaotic work and rather lacking in formal literary structure of the more classical type. If it is comparable to anything within the Western epic genre it is, perhaps, rather to the Italian romantic epics and the Arthurian romances. At times, however, particularly in Part 1, the Tibetan work seems to resemble nothing in Western literature so much as Blake's later 'Prophetic Books'. There is the same brilliant visual imagery, more Tibetan than Indian (the French translator, Gustave-Charles Toussaint, does not believe that there was a Sanskrit original for the work as claimed), the same visionary atmosphere, and the same ability to project the 'collective archetypes of the collective unconscious', both the terrible and the fascinating, in forms of hallucinatory vividness. Prosodically speaking the text consists mainly of long sequences of nine-syllable lines, with both longer and shorter lines also sometimes occurring. Changes of pace and mood are frequent. In the vigorous words of the French translator, 'Various tones follow each other in the incantation. It passes and repasses from dithyramb to macabre nightmare, from evocatory vertigo to objurgation, from a vehement and sombre realism to didactic dryness, but also to fervour, to the epic, to prophecy' (p. xxv).

The central event in Padmasambhava's life is his visit to Tibet, where he performed the celebrated feat of subduing the local gods and demons and participated in the consecration of the great temple-monastery of Samye. This historic visit took place in the reign of King Trisong Detsen (755-797 CE) and modern scholarship therefore regards Padmasambhava's career as being confined within the limits of the eighth century. The *Padma bKa'i Thang* takes a different view. While giving a full description of Padmasambhava's activities in Tibet, it sees the Precious Master's career as extending both forward into the distant future and backward into the remote past and as covering a period of altogether nearly three thousand years. The story begins in the land of Uddiyana. Amitabha, the Buddha of Boundless Light, emanates a ray of crimson radiance that falls upon a lotus in the Dhanakosha Lake, whereupon there appears seated on the calyx of the flower an eight year old child. This miraculous child, who is Padmasambhava, is adopted by Indrabhuti, the childless king of Uddiyana, and brought up as heir to the throne. Though married to a beautiful and virtuous princess he is mindful of his spiritual mission and wishing to renounce the kingdom gets himself exiled and, like the Buddha, leaves the palace on horseback. After performing austerities and mastering all manner of arts and sciences he receives ordination as a monk from Ananda, the disciple of the Buddha and his constant companion during the last years of his life. Ananda tells Padmasambhava of the Buddha's predictions, from which we learn that Padmasambhava was born forty-two years after the Parinirvana. Chronology is further dislocated by the fact that, according to Tibetan tradition, the Buddha was born not in 563 BCE (the generally accepted date) but several centuries earlier. Having received ordination Padmasambhava visits Kashmir, Nepal, Zahor, Khotan, and other places and stays in the eight great cremation grounds expounding the Dharma to the dakinis. He then goes to China, and learns astrological calculations from Manjushri, the Bodhisattva of Wisdom. In Zahor he meets the spiritually-minded princess Mandarava and accepts her as his disciple, whereupon her father, angry that the princess has consorted with a man, tries to burn him alive. Dakinis extinguish the flames of the pyre, and after seven days it is transformed into a lake of water and Padmasambhava appears in the form of an eight year old boy seated on a lotus and converts the king — an incident that is repeated, with variations, two or three times later in the story. Centuries passing, the Precious Master establishes the Dharma in Baiddha, Nepal, Serling (Sumatra?), Assam, Tukhara, and Persia, and his career becomes interwoven with the lives of such celebrated personages of Buddhist history as King Asoka — at whose prayer the genies build ten million stupas in a single night — and the teachers Nagarjuna and Aryadeva. There are also references, apparently anachronistic, to the persecution of Buddhists in Bengal and to the destruction of the great monastery of Vikramasila by the Hulagu Khan of Persia and of the shrines of Bodhgaya by the tirthikas or non-Buddhists under King Nagavishnu. Eventually, Padmasambhava receives King Trisong Detsen's invitation and travels to Tibet via Nepal, subduing the gods and demons as he goes, and forcing them to surrender their life-principle and swear an oath to protect the Dharma.

According to the *Padma bKa'i Thang's* reckoning Padmasambhava spent 111 years in Tibet. Samye being completed he and the 'Bodhisattva Abbot' Santarakshita perform the consecration ceremony to the accompaniment of many marvels, the king promulgates the code of laws which henceforth governs the social and religious life of Tibet, and the work of translating the Buddhist scriptures into the Tibetan language begins. Young Tibetans are trained as translators and, in the case of the most intrepid, go to India to study the Dharma. Indian monk-scholars are invited to Tibet. The most celebrated names in this connection are those of Vairotsana, who studies with twenty-five great Indian pandits, and Vimalamitra, who on his arrival in Tibet shows wonders, the story of each of them being related at some length over a number of cantos. Trisong Detsen having abolished the sanguinary Bon rites, the work of translation is brought to a successful conclusion, and despite strong opposition from the Bonists — due to whose machinations Vairotsana is banished and Vimalamitra slandered — the Dharma is at last established in Tibet. Secular works are also translated. The establishment of the Dharma is followed by the revision of the translations of the scriptures, after which the king recognizes the services of the translators and pandits with lavish gifts and most of them go home. In connection with these latter events, as well as with the death of Princess Pale Lotus, the king's daughter, Padmasambhava predicts the destruction of the monasteries and the slaughter of the monks and describes how, over a period of five thousand years, the teaching of the Buddha will grow and decline until the coming of the next Buddha, Maitreya. He also describes whereabouts in Tibet the termas or 'treasures' of texts and other objects which he has hidden for the benefit of future generations will be found, as well as the 'signs of the earth' and the times when these treasures will appear and who will discover them. The predictions having been made, King Trisong Detsen dies and Padmasambhava thinks of leaving Tibet but is persuaded to stay for three more years and makes more predictions and gives many teachings. In particular he addresses to the new king and to all the people of Tibet a lengthy exhortation which takes the form of an appallingly realistic description of the sufferings of the six realms of existence and of birth, old age, disease, and death. His mission in Tibet accomplished, the Precious Master mounts a marvellous winged horse, blue in colour, and accompanied by 'heroes of the four orders' and enveloped in rainbow-hued light leaves through the heavens for the land of the Rakshasas or cannibal demons — where, enthroned on the Copper-Coloured Mountain, he is still living and teaching.

No bare summary of the *Padma bKa'i Thang* can possibly do justice to the richness and diversity of its contents. Interwoven with the life of Padmasambhava, which of course is the principal theme, there are biographies of subordinate characters, descriptions of non-human beings, summaries of medical and astrological lore (in the latter the twelve nidanas and the months of the years are correlated with the Twelve Actions of the Buddha!), sublime spiritual teachings, ecstatic songs of praise, a guide book to Samye, catalogues of texts translated, and much else besides. As Tarthang Tulku writes in his Introduction, '[The *Padma bK'ai Thang*] is indeed a treasure, having the complexity and brilliance of a finely cut crystal, its facets the 108 cantos' (p. xxviii). Not that the crystal is perfectly symmetrical in shape, or that its facets are all equally well cut or of the same degree of brilliance! Nevertheless there is no doubt that, like the rainbow light that plays within the crystal, it is the magical figure of Padmasambhava that dominates the entire work, especially the central group of cantos, and it is the events described in these cantos, i.e. his visit to Tibet and his subjugation of the local gods and demons, that set the tone of the whole extraordinary narrative. In the earlier, Indian part of his three thousand year career Padmasambhava converts dakinis, kings, butchers, black magicians, and tirthikas, while one of the last things he does before leaving Tibet is to make a contract with the great demon king, King Pekar. Reading *The Life and Liberation of Padmasambhava* one gets the impression not only of a vivid and powerful spiritual 'personality' heroically battling with the forces of evil but also of a stream of impersonal spiritual energy which is conterminous with historical Buddhism itself and which, intervening in the course of events age after age, and assuming a variety of forms, brings under its control all the swirling emotional-psychic energies which at one or another level of mundane existence obstruct the liberating influence of the Dharma. This impression is heightened by the fact that Padmasambhava is actually involved in some of the most important events of Buddhist history, as well as by the fact that, at various stages of his career, he is known by different names. He has, we are told, eight secret names, eight borrowed names, eight present names, twenty magic names 'which vary at will', and so on. One indeed gets the impression that, perhaps extrapolating from Padmasambhava's exploits in Tibet, the text sees not only the history of Buddhism but the whole course of mundane existence in terms of a conflict between the forces of light and the forces of darkness — a conflict in which the forces of light are concerned not simply to conquer but to transmute and transform.

The most striking illustration of this almost Gnostic world-view occurs towards the beginning of the *Padma bKa'i Thang*, in the cantos describing the series of the births of the Rudra Tarpa Nagpo, or Black Salvation, and his subjugation by the Horse and the Swine, i.e. by the teacher Tubka Shunukyuwa, himself a form of Padmasambhava, and his disciple Den Pag, in the form of the horse-faced Vajrasattva and the swine-faced Vajrapani. The Rudra is a fallen monk, once a disciple of Tubka, who after myriads of existences in various evil and hideous forms is eventually reborn as a monster with three heads, six hands, four feet, two wings, and nine eyes. Feeding on the corpse of his mother, a prostitute who had been impregnated by three demons, he grows to enormous size and becomes the ruler of the demon kings who have seized control of the earth. Mad with pride, he fancies that there is none greater than he. The Horse and the Swine subjugate him by penetrating him through the rectum and the urethra and coming out of the top of his head, where they join each other. Tarpa Nagpo becomes the Dharma protector Mahakala, and is predicted to Buddhahood. He reappears later in the work, towards the end of the canto on 'The discourse on the Council of the Treasure, of the Law of the Treasure, of the Revealer of the Treasure' (Canto 53) where it is said, 'Although subdued, Rudra Tarpa Nagpo rises up again,' as though he represented, in his unregenerate form, a force which has to be subdued over and over again. In a remarkable passage the termas or 'treasures' are described as being hidden in various parts of his cosmic body, as if to suggest that the antidote to egotism is to be found in egotism itself — bodhi in the defilements, the Unconditioned in the conditioned. There is even a suggestion, elsewhere in the work, that the forces of light are actually strengthened by their conflict with the forces of darkness, and that one should, therefore, seek to learn from painful situations rather than run away from them. 'Hell is the lama of all the Buddhas' declares the Precious

Master, when asked by Prince Lhaje to exert his mercy and cut off the whole misery of the cycle of transmigration for himself and his parents.

Like much Tibetan Buddhist literature, the *Padma bKa'i Thang* is pervaded by a keen sense of the impermanence of all worldly things and a strong 'yearning faith' in The Three Jewels, commitment to which makes it possible for one not only to transcend the human predicament but also to become a stream of 'impersonal' spiritual energy working for the emancipation of all living beings. In additional to its vivid portrayal of Padmasambhava himself, and its powerful· dramatization of the conflict between the forces of light and the forces of darkness, the work also contains many important spiritual teachings, some of them being of a highly esoteric nature. Partly because they are not always explained in full, partly because of the literary rather than scholarly nature of the French translation, these are often difficult, even impossible, to understand. The general import of the work is nonetheless in no doubt whatever. Reading *The Life and Liberation of Padmasambhava* is a major imaginative and spiritual experience. This is due, principally, to the fact that 'the poetic beauty and symbolic strength of the Tibetan original' have been carried over from the French into the English translation, so that we can read this great work of literature in its present version not only for information but also for inspiration. Enjoyment and inspiration are alike enhanced by the reproductions of thankas which illustrate the material within the text, as well as by the care and devotion with which Tarthang Tulku and his co-workers at Dharma Publishing have produced these two splendid volumes. Holding them in our hands, we cannot but agree with Tarthang Tulku that Padmasambhava's teachings have now come to the West. We cannot but feel that Padmasambhava himself has now come to the West.

The Door of Liberation*

Geshe Wangyal is a Mongolian lama who studied at Drepung Monastery, near Lhasa, one of the three great Gelugpa monastic centres of Tibet. When I met him in Kalimpong in the early 'fifties, through the good offices of Marco Pallis, he was already proficient in English, having in fact spent some time in England before the war. In 1955 Geshe-la went to America, where he eventually founded Labsum Shedrup Ling (Lamaist Buddhist Monastery of America), the first Tibetan Buddhist monastery in that country. By the time I visited him there in 1970, when I was teaching at Yale, he had gathered around him a small band of serious-minded lay students of the Dharma who evidently valued the opportunity of sitting at the feet of a representative of the Tibetan Buddhist tradition who combined, to an unusual degree, profound learning, fervent devotion, and extreme simplicity of life.

The present volume is the outcome of Geshe Wangyal's work with these students. As an introductory note informs us, the translations of which it consists 'were taught to various disciples on different occasions, and over the years English versions of most were written down a number of times; this work was the foundation from which the present volume was prepared' (p. 10). In other words *The*

---

*Geshe Wangyal *The Door of Liberation* Prefatory note by H H The Dalai Lama. (New York: Maurice Girodias Associates, 1973)

Door of Liberation consists of *precepts*, i.e. of material selected by Geshe Wangyal from the vast mass of Tibetan Buddhist literature, canonical and non-canonical, in accordance with the spiritual needs of those who were studying with him. As such, it exemplifies the well known dictum of Atisa, in his reply to a question put to him on his arrival in Tibet: 'The precept of the Lama is more important than the scriptures and commentaries' (p. 121).

All the precepts thus selected have been taken, moreover, from works handed down in, or originating with, the spiritual lineage to which the translator himself belongs, i.e. the lineage of Atisa's chief disciple Geshe Drom, founder of the Khadampa School, and of Tsongkhapa, the founder of its continuation the Gelugpa School. Apart from the introduction, the work falls into two main parts. In the first part we have a short history of the lineage of the teaching, with accounts of Ananda, Upagupta, Nagarjuna, Aryadeva, Asanga, and other masters in the succession, together with stories illustrating workings of the law of karma. The first of these stories is a highly colourful account of the Miraculous Deeds of Sakyamuni Buddha, by means of which He gained victory over the Six Pandits, the second the romantic story of His previous life as Prince Gedun, and the third the unbelievably disastrous history of the nun Utpaladok. All these stories are paralleled in Pali canonical literature, and elsewhere.

The second part of the work consists entirely of material originating in Tibet. First comes a complete translation of the *Kadamthorbu*, or 'Precepts Collected from Here and There'. These precepts, which as the collector Tsun-ba-je-gom reminds us are 'the heartfelt speech of many holy beings', begin with short dialogues between Atisa and his closest disciples and are followed by the teachings of Drom and his later successors. Some of the precepts are very striking indeed. For example Yer-bay-shang-tsum tells us; 'If you do not meditate on impermanence in the early morning, by midday you will have many desires'. Next we have a group of four works by Tsongkhapa. The first is an ecstatic hymn of praise to the Buddha, as teacher of dependent origination, composed after a profound spiritual experience in which he had seen the true meaning of the Madhyamika teaching and obtained final insight into the nature of existence. The three other works are brief but systematic expositions of the Path from different points of view. The best known of the three is *The Three Principles of the Path,* an English version of which I produced some years ago with the help of John Driver at the special request of the Dalai Lama. Here it is accompanied by a commentary written by the Fourth Panchen Lama which firmly places the work within a context of spiritual practice in general and meditation practice in particular. All three works emphasize the importance of a total disengagement from conditioned existence, the development of the Will to Enlightenment, and the realization of Voidness through insight into the true meaning of dependent origination.

As one goes through the volume, one feels pervading every page a deep reverence for the Three Jewels, for the spiritual life, and the spiritual tradition. The actual production of the book, moreover, has evidently been carried out in the same spirit. Geshe Wangyal and his associates are deserving of our deepest gratitude for this gift of the Dharma, which places us in direct contact with one of the outstanding spiritual lineages of Tibetan Buddhism.

Visual Dharma and Aural Dharma*

Buddhist art has been known in the West almost as long as Buddhism, but it is only quite recently that its true nature, i.e. the nature of its relation to Buddhism and its place in the spiritual life, has begun to be understood. Formerly the function of Buddhist art was considered to be decorative, or at best illustrative. Buddhism (so it was thought) was essentially a system of abstract ideas, and these ideas were to be apprehended by the rational mind. The function of Buddhist art was to render the ideas more palatable, or to make them more easily comprehensible to the dull-witted. Buddhist art was thus of the nature of a concession, and in a better world would not have been necessary. Recently, however, a change has taken place, both in our understanding of Buddhism and our attitude towards Buddhist art. Indeed, the two are interrelated. Buddhism is now seen not as a system of abstract ideas, i.e. not just as a 'philosophy', but rather as a concrete spiritual experience. The abstract ideas are only the medium through which the experience is communicated. As for Buddhist art, it too is seen as a medium of communication — in its own right. Its function is not to illustrate the ideas in terms of which Buddhism, as a spiritual experience, is communicated to

*Chogyam Trungpa, Rinpoche *Visual Dharma: The Buddhist Art of Tibet* (Berkeley & London: Shambhala, 1975)

Piyadassi Thera *The Book of Protection* (Colombo: Mrs H M Gunasekera Trust, 1975)

the rational mind, but rather to act as an alternative means of communication altogether. Buddhist art communicates spiritual experience to the imagination through the medium of form and colour. It is visual Dharma. This more traditional attitude towards Buddhist art is exemplified in Chogyam Trungpa's book. *Visual Dharma: The Buddhist art of Tibet*, which is the catalogue of an exhibition of thangkas and images (mostly thangkas) held at the Massachusetts Institute of Technology, gives us not only a series of fifty-four plates, three of them in colour, but also descriptive notes on all the exhibits and an introductory essay that begins with the uncompromising statement 'The art of Tibet is entirely based on the spirituality of Buddhism'. Thus we get both a glimpse into the transcendental wonderland of Tibetan Buddhist art and a guide to its true significance. The introductory essay is divided into three parts: Background and History, Elements of Iconography, and Five Buddha Families. In the second of these, which is of particular interest and value, the Rinpoche tells us that thangkas and other forms of Tibetan art express the vision of tantric Buddhism and that they fall, according to their subject matter, into six general categories: (1) enlightened beings (i.e. buddhas, gurus, and bodhisattvas), (2) yidams, (3) dharmapalas, (4) mandalas and stupas, (5) illustrations of the teaching, and (6) yantras. Accounts are given of all of these, the greatest amount of space being devoted to the yidams or personal deities. 'A practitioner's yidam represents his particular characteristic expression of buddha-nature. Identifying with his yidam, therefore, means identifying with his own basic nature, free from its distorted aspects' (p. 20). Many of the illustrations depict yidams, and this tells us a great deal not only about the Tantra but about the Buddhist art of Tibet.

As visual Dharma, Buddhist art directs itself to the sense of sight, for it is sight that perceives form and colour, the medium through which Buddhist art communicates with the imagination. In addition to the sense of sight, however, there is another highly developed sense, that of hearing. Buddhist art therefore communicates not only through the medium of form and colour but through the medium of sound. In addition to visual Dharma there is aural Dharma. This aural Dharma consists in instrumental music (such as that which accompanies many Tibetan ceremonies) and chanting. When it consists of chanting there must, of course, be something chanted. What is this? In Sri Lanka at least, the answer would be, more often then not, that it is the *Pirith Potha* or 'Book of Protection', and it is this which Piyadassi Thera has translated from the original Pali with an introductory essay and explanatory notes. Originally compiled for the use of novice monks, the work is, the translator tells us, the most widely known Pali book in Sri Lanka (Ceylon), and can be called the Buddhist Bible(!). It consists for the most part of twenty-four short texts selected from the Sutta Piṭaka of the Pali Canon, and the nature of the selection tells us a good deal about the general character of traditional Sinhalese Buddhism. Besides the well known Mangala, Ratana, and Karaniyametta Suttas, there are spiritual instructions like the three discourses on the factors of Enlightenment (*bojjhanga*), practical advice like the ten verses on the Advantages of Friendship, ancient legends like the Discourse at Isigili, 'magical' and 'mythical' material like the Maha Samaya or 'Great Assembly' Discourse, social comment like the Discourse on Outcastes, and profound 'philosophical' expositions like the Discourse on the Analysis of the (Four Noble) Truths (*saccavibhanga*). With one or two exceptions all these discourses were traditionally ascribed to the Buddha. In the present context, however, we are concerned not so much with the contents of the texts as with the use that is made of them.

Piyadassi Thera tells us that it is the practice, in Buddhist lands, to listen to the recital of the dhamma or doctrine of the Buddha 'in order to avert illness or danger, to ward off the influence of malignant beings, to obtain protection and deliverance from evil, and to promote health, prosperity, welfare, and well-being' (p. 11). How the recital is able to do this he explains partly with the help of modern tradition and partly with the help of modern discoveries in the field of parapsychology. He also gives us a description of the way in which the paritta — or in Sinhalese pirith — ceremony is performed in Sri Lanka. It is clear, however, that the true significance of paritta transcends any purely rationalistic explanation, and that it is most effective when, with concentrated mind, the devotee makes himself completely receptive to the spiritual reality which is behind the words as recited. Paritta thus becomes aural Dharma. Should a further edition of *The Book of Protection* be called for, the author may consider it worth his while to include the Pali texts of the suttas in Roman character. As he himself points out, 'the habit of listening to the recital of Paritta suttas among Westerners is growing' (p. 18), and it would be helpful if material of this kind was more widely available.

Thirty Years of Buddhist Studies*

The name of Dr Edward Conze requires no introduction to any English-knowing person with an interest in Buddhism. Since 1951 he has given us a steady stream of original works on Buddhism and translations of Buddhist texts, the majority of them marked by thoroughness of scholarship, distinction of thought and style, wide range of literary and philosophical reference, an agreeable tartness of expression, and an all-pervading spiritual concern. The present volume, his seventeenth dealing with Buddhism according to my reckoning, garners some of the chips from his workshop over the last three decades.

As might have been expected, the essays comprising *Thirty Years of Buddhist Studies* (a slightly misleading title, perhaps) reflect most of the author's major interests. Seven of them deal, in one way or another, with the Prajñāpāramitā or 'Perfection of Wisdom' tradition, one of them consisting of a translation of 'The Perfection of Wisdom in Seven Hundred Lines' hitherto available only in typescript and duplicated form. Others deal with Mahayana Buddhism, with Recent Progress in Buddhist Studies, and with Buddhist Philosophy and its European parallels, both genuine and spurious. For good measure, there is one on the Meditation on Death as well as a translation of Saddharma-puṇḍarīka Chapter 5 which

Thirty Years of Buddhist Studies: Selected Essays by Edward Conze (Bruno Cassirer, 1967)

makes us very much wish that Dr Conze would give us (as I suggested to him some years ago) a complete version of this important Sutra. Surely he is not going to leave us indefinitely to the tender mercies of Kern and Soothill!

Despite the severely intellectual and technical nature of much of the material with which he deals, Dr Conze's concern for Buddhism as a living spiritual tradition breaks through whenever it finds an opportunity. Some of his comments are particularly relevant to the Western Buddhist scene. Speaking of Prof. T. R. V. Murti's *The Central Philosophy of Buddhism* he says, 'Its title is a challenge to Western Buddhists which so far they show little sign of heeding, with the result that their faulty perspective vitiates both their theory and practice. The central tradition is that of Emptiness, represented by the Sarvastivadins, Madyamikas, and Tibetan Lamas. By contrast, Theravadins and Zen, which alone have caught on so far, are peripheral' (pp. 20-21). Even more acidly, 'Zen was designed to operate within emptiness. When coming West it transferred into a vacuum' (p. 29). Himself an intellectual, he is deeply aware of the limitations of a purely theoretical approach to Buddhism, and reminds us, 'It is up to us to see to it that the rain which has descended so abundantly from the Rain-cloud of the dharma actually nourishes our spiritual faculties, and does not just go down the drain of mere intellectual curiosity' (p. 32). Finally there is a word of advice to would-be Bodhisattvas. 'A very high degree of sanctity is necessary to do good to others without harming or irritating them' (p. 58). The volume would be well worth buying simply for the sake of *aperçus* such as these.

Forty Years in the Workshop*

More than thirty-five years ago I carried home from a second hand bookshop in south London the four stout volumes of Max Muller's *Chips from a German Workshop*, and I can still remember the thrill of pleasure they gave me. It is with no less pleasure, and even greater profit, that I explored the second volume of 'chips' from the good German workshop which Dr Conze set up on British soil in 1933 with, as he tells us, no other capital than 'a fairly large work on *Der Satz vom Widerspruch* which, modelling myself a bit on Arthur Schopenhauer, I was inclined to regard as my *Hauptwerk*' (p. ix).

Like his great predecessor Dr Conze writes a fluent and readable English of some literary distinction, and we are reminded that English is not his native tongue by little more than the fact that he writes it more correctly than the educated Englishman normally would do. In the extent of his range, too, he resembles Max Muller, and if there is less philology, and more psychology, in the *Studies* than in the *Chips*, the general reader, at least, will not complain. Like Max Muller, too, Dr Conze has been occupied for the greater part of his working life with a single major literary project. In Max Muller's case this was, of course, the editing and translating of the *Rig Veda*, and many of the 'chips' in my four stout volumes were, I found, the by-

*Further Buddhist Studies: Selected Essays by Edward Conze (Oxford: Bruno Cassirer, 1975)

products of this great undertaking. Similarly, Dr Conze has for thirty years and more devoted himself to editing, translating, and elucidating the corpus of Mahayana sutras, approximately three dozen in number, which deal with Prajñāpāramitā or Perfect Wisdom, and which together constitute, as he has more than once reminded us, one of the greatest outbursts of spiritual creativity in the history of mankind. Both in *Further Buddhist Studies* and in its predecessor *Thirty Years of Buddhist Studies* some of Dr Conze's biggest and most important chips are a by-product of his heroic labours at this colossal task, labours which have resulted in what is, with the possible exception of the Pali Text Society's translations of the Sutta- and Vinaya-Piṭakas of the Pali Canon, probably the biggest single contribution to the English-speaking world's knowledge of the Buddhist scriptures.

The essays brought together in the present volume are distributed under four headings: (1) Longer Articles, (2) The Philosophical Background, (3) Shorter Articles, and (4) Reviews; and they range backwards and forwards over the fields of philosophy, psychology, logic, comparative religion, sociology, history, and the fine arts. Now Dr Conze is examining an eleventh century Sanskrit manuscript, now exploring the social origins of nominalism, now casting doubt on the ability of 'Analytical Psychology' to do justice to the higher ranges of the spiritual life. Out of the riches thus placed at our disposal, probably it is the three longer articles that will have the greatest appeal to the English-speaking Western Buddhist, particularly the third, 'Love, Compassion, and Sympathetic Joy', in which we see Dr Conze at his most caustic and most acute. To me the most interesting of the essays, in many ways, is the second of the longer articles, 'Buddhism and Gnosis'. In this essay, originally a paper read at a learned congress on The Origins of Gnosticism,

Dr Conze describes what he thinks are the eight basic similarities between Near-eastern Gnosis and Indian Mahayana Buddhism. Though I have long felt that there was some connection, not necessarily a historical one, between Buddhism and Gnosticism, on the whole I find Dr Conze's similarities not very convincing — possibly because the discussion is not exhaustive enough to be conclusive. In particular, the discussion of Wisdom as a feminine deity seems to require, in the case of Mahayana Buddhism at least, rather more than the rash application of the vague and uncritical distinction between 'matriarchal' and 'patriarchal' religions. Most uncharacteristically, Dr Conze would seem to have fallen victim here to the methods of 'Analytical Psychology'.

The three articles that make up 'The philosophical Background' are the product of Dr Conze's Marxist studies, having been decanted into English, as he tells us in the foreword, from the original German of *Der Satz vom Widerspruch*. Not very surprisingly, they all foreshadow to some extent certain of his later preoccupations in the field of Buddhist thought. Consideration of the objective validity of that bedrock of formal logic the principle of contradiction, for instance, leads him from the dialectics of Heracleitus, Nicholas of Cusa, and Hegel straight into the transcendental domain of Perfect Wisdom, wherein all the laws of thought are suspended, and so to thirty years of work on the Prajñāpāramitā sutras. Despite early ascetical and mystical leanings, Dr Conze must sometimes have asked himself how the author of a Schopenhaurian *Hauptwerk* could ever have ended up in this way. The atmosphere of the 'Shorter Articles' is on the whole much less rarified, and in most of them we find ourselves on what is, conventionally speaking, firmer ground. Indeed, in 'The present State and future Prospects of Buddhism in Asia' Dr Conze brings us back to earth with a nasty bump.

How many Western Buddhists, I wonder, realize how great has been the damage suffered by Buddhist institutions in Asia, and the extent to which the pressure of modern life affects monastic institutions, doctrinal integrity, and co-operation between monks and laity? Dr Conze indeed goes so far as to speak of 'the deadly and irreconcilable conflict between Buddhist traditions and the main forces of the modern age' (p. 126), and I do not think he exaggerates. In the 'Reviews', where we are given a mere 31 out of a total of 143 actually written and published, we are very much in the workshop, and the chips fly thick and fast as Dr Conze, axe in hand, gives a keen and workmanlike appraisal of the products of other workshops, these latter being largely in the form of editions and translations of Sanskrit Buddhist texts and expositions of the Dharma both scholarly and popular. Sometimes the sparks fly too, for Dr Conze finds some of the products extremely shoddy. Arthur Koestler's *The Lotus and the Robot* is shown to be 'a mere travesty of the facts', while the author of *Philosophy of the Buddha*, A. J. Bahm, is convicted of total ignorance of his subject. Where praise is due, however, Dr Conze can be both warm and generous, and in the fairly numerous instances where the workmanship is of uneven quality, or the product only partly satisfactory, he deals out praise and blame with judicial impartiality.

In this volume, which jointly with its predecessor the publishers rightly describe as representing 'an almost inexhaustible source for all serious students of Buddhism', Dr Conze throughout shows himself very much the scholar, indeed, very much the German scholar — thorough, conscientious, and painstaking, and in all that concerns his chosen field of study well-informed to the point of virtual omniscience. At the same time he reveals himself to be very much a Buddhist. In the foreword where he has, so he rather engagingly confesses, at the prompting of friends let his hair down 'quite a bit', he tells us that during the war he devoted himself to the practice of meditation first in a wood in Hampshire, then in a caravan in Oxfordshire. In the eyes of some scholars so 'unscientific' an approach totally disqualifies him from writing on Buddhism, and it is clear that, in Dr Conze's own words, some of his views stick in the gullets of his academic contemporaries. Indeed, his acceptance of magic induced the then president of the Aristotlean Society, who was also the first female professor of logic in modern history, to absent herself from the meeting where she should have chaired his paper on 'Dharma as a spiritual, social, and cosmic Force'. Having had my own experience of the workings of this kind of logic, I feel I can share Dr Conze's amusement. Quite recently a translation of one of my books was refused by a European-language publisher on the grounds that the author was a Buddhist and could not, therefore, be objective about Buddhism. Eventually he decided to publish, instead, a translation of a book by Alan Watts. So far as Western Buddhists are concerned, — so far as Buddhists everywhere are concerned, — whether the author be a scholar who has meditated or a monk who tries not to be unscholarly a book on Buddhism is none the worse for having been written by someone who actually believes in the Dharma. Indeed, they will rejoice that a scholar of Dr Conze's standing should say such things as 'there is no greater menace than a mere grammarian let loose on a sacred text' (p. 138), not to mention *aperçus* like 'a religion's unworldliness is its greatest asset' (p. 179) and 'It is foolish to expect too much advance information about spiritual states' (p. 149).

Apart from the fact that it written by one who is both pandita and upasaka, scholar and devotee, one of the strongest impressions that one gets from this book is that of continuity and completeness of development. From the

Teutonic lucubrations of *Der Satz vom Widerspruch* to the genial asperity of the latest book reviews, the themes with which Dr Conze is preoccupied remain constant. Nor is this all. Despite the difficulties with which he has had to contend, he has had the satisfaction not only of having throughout his career

> . . . *wrought*
> *Upon the plan that pleased his boyish thought*

but also of being able to carry to a successful conclusion one of the most important literary undertakings in the history of Western Buddhism. Indeed, now that he has given us *The Larger Sutra of Perfect Wisdom* (1976), it would appear that (apart from the unfinished translation of the *Saddharma-puṇḍarīka* Sutra?) Dr Conze's *biographia literaria* has no loose ends left, and it is perhaps significant that he rounds off *Further Buddhist Studies* with a bibliography. After forty years in the workshop, who will blame him if he wishes to lay down his tools at last and retire, if not to the wood in Hampshire or the caravan in Oxfordshire, at least to some quiet retreat in the depths of rural Dorset, there to adopt again, perhaps, the more direct approach to the great truths which he has served so faithfully and so long.

D. H. Lawrence and the Spiritual Community*

D. H. Lawrence died at Vence, in the south of France, on 2nd March 1930, at the age of forty-four. In the course of twenty years of writing life he had produced a substantial body of work that comprised fiction, poetry, travel-writing, essays, criticism, history, reminiscence, letters, reviews, and plays, as well as paintings. A considerable portion of this output occupies an important place in twentieth century English literature, and some of it — mainly fiction and poetry, undoubtedly ranks as a permanent part of our literary heritage. In the decade following his death Lawrence's reputation as a writer declined, but in more recent years it has steadily increased and he is now widely regarded as the outstanding creative force of his generation. It was therefore to be expected that the fiftieth anniversary of his death should be marked by the production of radio and television versions of his novels, revivals of his plays, and, of course, the publication of books on the man himself, his life, and his work.

Among the books that have so far appeared is this illustrated biography by Keith Sagar, already well known as the editor of *Lawrence's Selected Poems* in the Penguin Poets series. Glossy, large, and lavishly illustrated as it is, it would be easy to dismiss *The Life of D. H. Lawrence* as yet another 'coffee table' volume; but the book is in fact much

---

*Keith Sagar *The Life of D. H. Lawrence: An Illustrated Biography.* (Eyre Methuen, 1980)

more than that. As any biography of Lawrence must, it of course takes us from the township in the semi-rural, semi-industrialized Midlands where 'Young Bert' grew up, to the villa on the Côte D'Azur where, 'The Longest Journey' ended, the famous — perhaps notorious — author died of tuberculosis. In between we are taken to London and Cornwall, Germany and Italy, New Mexico, Ceylon, and Australia. We meet intellectuals and aristocrats, writers and artists, peasants and peons, bohemians and bankers.

But although we are taken on the usual biographical conducted tour, we are not taken on it in quite the usual way. What Mr Sagar has done is both novel and interesting. He has told the story of Lawrence's life mainly by means of extracts from Lawrence's own writings, especially the letters, as well as from the letters, diaries, and reminiscences of his friends. Mr Sagar himself provides the connecting narrative. In this way we are given a sort of running commentary on the events of Lawrence's life more or less as they actually happen, and given it, for the most part, in Lawrence's own words and the words of those who, for a longer or a shorter period, were in personal contact with him and who were themselves a part of his life. The result of this method is a tremendous immediacy of impact. We seem to be living *with* Lawrence rather than reading about him long afterwards. The impression of immediacy is heightened by the fact that the text is accompanied throughout with 150 pictures, many of them not previously published, which are almost as essential to the book as the text itself. These pictures enable us to see the places in which Lawrence lived, and the people with whom he associated. They enable us to see the physical changes that took place in him over the years. It is indeed with something like a shock that we see the handsome, healthy young man of twenty-three slowly turning into the haggard, shrunken figure of forty-four.

Sixteen of the pictures are in colour, eight of them being reproductions of Lawrence's own paintings. The colours of the paintings tell us something about Lawrence that we could not, perhaps, have learned in any other way.

By permitting Lawrence's life to speak, virtually, for itself, Keith Sagar enables us to see a number of things that might otherwise have remained obscure. I for one am convinced that what killed Lawrence was not so much tuberculosis as the war. Keith Sagar himself seems to believe as much. In the introduction to his Penguin *Selected Poems* he says, 'The horrors of the war, the moral debacle at home, the suppression of his splendid novel, *The Rainbow*, persecution, ill-health, and poverty, all combined to destroy in Lawrence, during the war, his faith in humanity and a human future'. As early as 1915 Lawrence stated bluntly, 'The War finished me: it was the spear through the side of all sorrows and hopes' (p. 75), while towards the end of his life he told Trigant Burrow that his illness was nothing but chagrin caused by 'the absolute frustration of my primeval societal instinct' (p. 218) and Witter Bynner that his sickness was 'a sort of rage' (p. 242). The war was, indeed, a kind of watershed in his life. Between the pre-war and the post-war Lawrence there is a whole world of difference. The first was the man of whom Jessie Chambers wrote, 'Lawrence seemed so happy that merely to be alive and walking about was an adventure, and his gift for creating an atmosphere of good fellowship a joy' (p. 26); the second the man who, at thirty, described himself as being 'mad with misery and hostility and rage' (p. 85), and who wrote, 'Sometimes I wish I could let go and be really wicked — kill and murder — but kill chiefly. I do want to kill. But I want to select whom I shall kill. Then I shall enjoy it' and, 'I am hostile, hostile, hostile to all that is, in our public and national life. I want to destroy it' (p. 86). The first Lawrence did not, of course, die completely,

— in a sense he even outlived the second Lawrence, — and in the end attained a kind of wan resurrection. Mr Sagar is not quite correct, however, in saying that, during the war, Lawrence's faith in humanity and a human future was destroyed. What happened was that his faith took a more specialized, a more desperate, form. It took a form that was, in effect, a response to the challenge of the war. It took the form of what Lawrence called Rananim and what Buddhists call Sangha or Spiritual Community.

This is not to say that there is much in Mr Sagar's biography that is of direct Buddhist interest, though there is much that is of indirect Buddhist interest, as least so far as Western Buddhists are concerned. Lawrence's references to Buddhism are few, and most of them are uncomplimentary. To Earl and Achsah Brewster, Americans, vegetarians, and 'budding Buddhists' as Richard Aldington called them, whom he had met in Capri in 1921 and with whom he joined up in Ceylon for a few weeks the following year, on his way to Australia, Lawrence wrote 'The American Indian, the Aztec, old Mexico — all that fascinates me and has fascinated me for years. *There* is glamour and magic for me. Not Buddha. Buddha is so finished and perfected and fulfilled and *vollendet*, and without any new possibilities — to me I mean' (pp. 128-129). In Ceylon itself, where Earl Brewster was studying Pali, his impressions of Buddhism were even less favourable, though he enjoyed the Kandy Perahera, which was 'wonderful, gorgeous and barbaric with all its elephants and flames and devil dances in the night'. Not without insight, in view of the fact that it is the Theravada Buddhism of Ceylon on which he is commenting, he continues, 'One realizes how barbaric the substratum of Buddhism is. I shrewdly suspect that the high-flownness of Buddhism altogether exists mostly on paper: and that its denial of the soul makes it always rather barren, even if philosophically, etc., it is more perfect'. He concludes, 'In short, after a slight contact, I draw back and don't like it' (p. 130). He certainly did not like what, writing to another friend, he described as 'the nasty faces and yellow robes of the Buddhist monks, the little vulgar dens of the temples' (p. 130), but then the heat that year was exceptional even for Ceylon, Lawrence was ill all the time he was there, and when he wrote he was evidently in a bad mood. Later, from Australia, he wrote to Earl Brewster, 'How I *hated* a great deal of my time in Ceylon: never felt so sick in my life. Yet now it is a very precious memory, invaluable. Not wild horses would drag me back. But neither time nor eternity will take away what I have of it: Ceylon and the East' (pp. 130-131). It is interesting to speculate what might have been the result had Lawrence come into contact with a form of Buddhism more spiritually alive that the Theravada Buddhism of Ceylon. What would he have made of Zen, for instance, or of Tibetan Buddhism, had they been more accessible in his day? What would he have thought of our own Movement, had he lived long enough to see it? Despite his unfavourable opinion of Buddhism, or what purported to be Buddhism, there is little doubt that some of the questions with which he was most deeply concerned were questions on which Buddhism had some-thing of special value to say to him. It is therefore important that Buddhists, especially Western Buddhists, should not be misled by Lawrence's bad-tempered snarlings at monks and temples but try to understand what he meant by Rananim and why his efforts to establish it were unsuccessful.

'Ra'annanim' is a Hebrew word meaning 'green, fresh, and flourishing', and Keith Sagar tells us that 'Rananim was to be a monastic community secluded from the sick world, of some twenty righteous or at least like-minded people dedicated to fostering 'new shoots of life' within themselves, and subsequently to seeding the sterile ruins of Western civilization' (p. 75). The similarity to our own conception of Spiritual Community is obvious. At one time Lawrence referred to Rananim as the 'island' idea, adding, 'But they say, the island shall be England, that we shall start our new community in the midst of the old one, as a seed falls among the roots of the parent' (p. 83). (There are overtones here of Blake's building Jerusalem in England's green and pleasant land, but Lawrence seems to be unconscious of them.) At another time it was 'the colony', and it was to be in Florida — or Cornwall (p. 94). Once the idea took the still more tenuous form of founding a publishing company 'that publishes for the sake of truth' (p. 97). According to Keith Sagar, Lawrence had long been fascinated by the monastic life. 'Despite his allegiance to the body, he led a very simple, slightly ascetic life, and his hatred of the human |as distinct from the animal and vegetable| world led him to explore various forms of withdrawl from it. He often spoke of Rananim as a "monastic community" '(p. 117). (Buddhist monasticism is not, of course, based on hatred of the human world.) On at least one occasion, towards the end of his life, when he had given up hope of being able to establish Rananim, he advised the young Rolf Gardiner to found what — using an interesting expression — he called 'flexible monasteries' (p. 206). In one form or another, the idea of Rananim was, according to Keith Sagar, 'always Lawrence's last resort. All his other ideas about human relationships were put to the test, if not in reality, then in his fiction. But he never dared follow through, imaginatively, the Rananim idea; it was too precious to put at risk. When he writes of it in his letters, his language lapses into Arcadian or Prelapsarian' (p. 104).

Reluctant as he may have been to follow the Rananim idea through imaginatively, in his fiction (as Goethe, for instance, had done, with a similar idea, in *Wilhelm Meister's*

Travels) Lawrence certainly strove to bring it into existence as a concrete social reality, at least during the decade from 1914 to 1924, and at least intermittently. In 1915 he was doing his best to co-opt such Cambridge-Bloomsbury figures as E. M. Forster and Bertrand Russell, as well as John Middleton Murry and the young Aldous Huxley. In 1925 came the famous party at the Café Royal when, a few days after his return from America, Lawrence asked his seven special friends, one by one, if they would go with him (and Frieda Lawrence) back to New Mexico and start a new life, and when only the deaf artist Dorothy Brett — accompanied by Toby, her ear trumpet, — actually did so. In between, he and Murry started up a little monthly paper and organized weekly meetings, both of which soon fizzled out, he and Murry swore bloodbrotherhood (or at least Lawrence did), and the Lawrences and the Murrys tried to live together in Cornwall. Perhaps the nearest Lawrence ever came to realizing his idea of Rananim was when, in 1922, he and Frieda lived for four months in New Mexico very close to the two itinerant young Danish artists, Knud Merrild and Kai Gótzsche. 'The Lawrences and the Danes made no demands on each other,' says Keith Sagar, 'and an easy friendship developed spontaneously' (p. 146). In the end Lawrence was reduced to projecting his idea of Rananim onto the lives of the ancient Etruscans who, provided one did not look too closely, could be regarded as having created a perfect human society — a society that had been destroyed by the brutal militaristic Romans.

Seeing how desperately Lawrence believed in the idea of Rananim, — *needed* to believe if he was to retain any faith in humanity and a human future, — the question that confronts us is, Why was Lawrence unable to give concrete, social embodiment to his idea? Why was he unable to establish Rananim as a living reality? After all, besides being, as a writer, the outstanding creative force of his generation, as a man he was, by all accounts, an exceptionally charming and stimulating companion. Yet towards the end of 1916, looking back over what was to have been the Year One of the New World, he could write to Koteliansky, from whose chanting of Hebrew music he had taken the word Rananim, 'I tell you Rananim, my Florida idea, was the true one. Only the *people* were wrong. But to go to Rananim *without* the people is right.' On which Keith Sagar wryly comments, 'a colony without people. A sad conclusion' (p. 100). A sad conclusion indeed! A colony, — a Rananim, — a spiritual community, — consisting, in effect, of just Lawrence and Frieda! What had gone wrong? What was it that *continued* to go wrong, and continued to go wrong until, even though he so passionately believed that 'Men are free when they belong to a living, organic, *believing* community, active in fulfilling some unfulfilled, perhaps unrealized purpose' (p. 145), — even though he complained so bitterly of the frustration of his primeval societal instinct ('societal' perhaps in a deeper sense that he knew), — Rananim in the end became no more than a dream and Lawrence could write to Ralph Gardiner, resignedly now, but still sadly, 'As far as anything *matters*, I have always been very much alone, and regretted it' ? (p. 206).

What had gone wrong was not one thing, but a number of things, all iterrelated. In the light of our own experience of spiritual community, within the FWBO, it may be possible for us not only to identify the principal factors leading to the failure of Lawrence's idea of Rananim but also to make it clear how, given those factors, the idea was doomed to failure from the start. We can best do this, perhaps, by first reminding ourselves of some basic principles, — principles that, as a result of our own efforts to put the Buddhist ideal of Spiritual Community into practice in the West, we have found to be true, — and then applying those principles to the idea of Rananim, as Lawrence actually sought to carry it out. Enumerated more or less at random, the principles in question are: (1) The spiritual community consists of individuals. (2) The 'couple' is the enemy of the spiritual community. (3) The spiritual community is not a group. (4) The spiritual community must have a common ideal and a common method of practice. Though enumerated at random, these four principles will provide us with a framework for a brief discussion of Lawrence's failure to give concrete, social embodiment to his idea of Rananim and, at the same time, enable us to see the limitations of the idea of Rananim itself — limitations that were obvious to at least some of Lawrence's friends, even though they were not all obvious to all of them, or even to Lawrence himself.

(1) *The spiritual community consists of individuals.* The significance of this statement is not so obvious as it might, at first sight, appear to be. What do we mean by 'individuals', and in what way does a spiritual community consist of them? At least so far as the establishing of Rananim was concerned, Lawrence himself it seems did not have a clearly defined concept of 'the individual', - perhaps would not have wanted to have one, — although when he told Koteliansky 'only the *people* were wrong,' what he may have meant was that they were not individuals, i.e. not true individuals. From the Buddhist point of view, the (true) individual is one who is self-conscious or self-aware (though not in the alienated way that Lawrence so rightly condemned), able to think for himself, emotionally positive, creative rather than reactive in his attitude towards life, spontaneous, sensitive, and responsible. The spiritual community consists of (true) individuals in the sense that it is a free association of — the sum total of the non-exploitive, non-addictive relationships between — a number of people who are individuals in the

sense defined. Lawrence perhaps had an inkling of what this sort of community was like when, towards the end of his life, he wrote that 'the new relationship will be some sort of tenderness, sensitive, between men and men and men and women, and not the one up one down, lead on I follow, *ich dien* sort of business' (p. 207).

(2) *The 'couple' is the enemy of the spiritual community.* By the couple, in this context, one means two people, usually of the opposite sex, who are neurotically dependent on each other and whose relationship, therefore, is one of mutual exploitation and mutual addiction. A couple consists, in fact, of two half-people, each of whom unconsciously invests part of his or her total being in the other: each is dependent on the other for the kind of psychological security that can be found, ultimately, only within oneself. Two such half-people, uneasily conjoined as a couple, can no more be part of a spiritual community than Siamese twins can be part of the *corps de ballet*. Their 'presence' within the spiritual community can only have a disruptive effect. The couple is therefore the enemy of the spiritual community. Lawrence, however, did not see this. Perhaps, because of his personal history, and the pervasive influence of our culturally-conditioned notion of 'romantic love' between the sexes, he *could* not see it. As is well known, for him the man-woman relationship was at the very centre of things, even though balanced, to some extent, by the man-man relationship. This meant, in effect, that the couple was at the centre of things. Rananim was to be made up of married couples: a contradiction in terms. Among all Lawrence's friends, the only person who seems to have spotted the contradiction was E. M. Forster. Writing at the beginning of 1915, after Lawrence had scolded him so much on his visits to Greatham that, as Keith Sagar says, 'at last the worm turned', he began his letter, 'Dear Lawrences,' and continued, significantly, 'Until you think it

worthwhile to function separately, I'd better address you as one . . .' (p. 82). Because Lawrence did not think it 'worthwhile' to function separately it was not really possible for him to relate to others *as an individual*, — certainly not to the extent that is required in the spiritual community, — and because he could not relate to others as an individual he was unable to bring Rananim into existence. He could not have his wedding cake and eat it too, although, like most of us, he wanted to.

(3) *The Spiritual Community is not a group.* It is not a group because a group, unlike a spiritual community, does not consist of individuals but of those who have yet to become individuals. Before one can distinguish the spiritual community from the group, therefore, one must be able to distinguish the individual from the proto-individual or 'group member', and in order to do that one must be an individual oneself, for only an individual can recognize another individual. From this it follows that if one is not an individual, and therefore unable to distinguish individual from proto-individual, one will tend to bring into existence not a spiritual community but, at best, a 'positive group'. This is what happened with Lawrence. Moreover, if one is not able to relate to others as an individual one will tend to relate to them in some other way. Lawrence was not able to relate to others as an individual: he had to be their leader; he had to ask them to follow him. Most of his friends did not want to do this, much as they loved and admired him, and some of them were honest enough to say so. 'I like you Lawrence,' said Mary Cannan, when *she* was asked if she would go with him back to New Mexico, 'but not so much as all that, and I think you are asking what no human being has a right to ask another' (pp. 168-169). Eventually, Lawrence himself repudiated the idea of leadership, as we have seen, declaring, 'the leader of men is a back number' (p. 207). He had seen that Rananim could not be a group;

but he had not really seen how it could be a spiritual community. He could not 'link up with the social unconscious,' i.e. could not be simply a member of the group; at the same time, not being a true individual, he was unable to enter into a free association with other individuals, even had he been able to find them. Consequently, 'One has no real human relations — that is so devastating' (p.218).

(4) *The Spiritual Community must have a common ideal and a common method of practice.* As we have seen, the spiritual community consists of individuals. But individuals, i.e. true individuals, do not come ready made: they have to be created; they have to create themselves. A spiritual community, therefore, cannot be established in the sort of way that a group can be established. It comes into existence only when a number of people work on themselves — and on one another — in such a way that they actually become individuals and are able to relate to one another as individuals. But how does one work on oneself? How does one actually become an individual? In order to become an individual one needs a definite method of practice, by which is meant not a mere technique of bringing about 'results' irrespective of one's mental attitude but an effective means of radical self-transformation. In Buddhism the principal method of practice is meditation, in which one works directly on the mind itself, transforming self-consciousness into transcendental consciousness and so on. Lawrence wanted to establish Rananim. But he and his friends were not individuals to start with, though Lawrence himself, at least, had some of the characteristics of the true individual, nor were they able to work on themselves and become individuals. They were unable to work on themselves because they had no common method of practice. All that Lawrence was able to offer them was the prospect of somehow reverting to the

pre-conscious state of the infant, in which self-consciousness does not exist and one feels at one with the whole of existence — thus implying that the pre-conscious state is higher then the conscious state. Moreover, a definite method of practice presupposes a definite ideal, for a method is a method only in relation to a certain end. Since Lawrence had no clearly defined concept of the individual it was not really possible for him to have the individual as his ideal, and because he did not have the individual as his ideal it was not possible for him and his friends to become individuals, or even to have a means of becoming such. In Buddhism the end in relation to which meditation is the principal means is true individuality. The ultimate ideal of Buddhism is the ideal of human enlightenment, which is not an ideal imposed upon man from without (the kind of pseudo-ideal against which Lawrence protested) but one which is implicit in his own nature and which represents the fulfillment of his nature in the deepest and truest sense.

Lawrence's idea of Rananim was much more than one sensitive, creative person's response to the challenge of war. In reality it represented the proto-individual's response to the challenge of the group as such, whether in peace or war, a response that in Lawrence's case took the form of an attempt — a blind, almost instinctive attempt — to rise from the level of the group to a higher level of human development, both individual and collective, by establishing the kind of new society that Buddhists call Sangha or Spiritual Community. Unfortunately, for the reasons that have been given, Lawrence's attempt to give concrete, social embodiment to his idea of Rananim was a failure. For us that failure is not without its uses, especially at a time like the present, when the brute mass of corporate existence by which we are surrounded — in which we live embedded — poses a greater threat, and presents a greater challenge, than it ever did in Lawrence's time. Among other things, Lawrence's failure serves to remind us that the spiritual community is something that has to be striven for. The fact that the ideal of Sangha or Spiritual Community is an integral part of Buddhism does not mean that spiritual community comes to us on a plate. It is not something that, as 'Buddhists', we automatically have. On the contrary, it is something we bring into existence from moment to moment by virtue of our free association one with another as individuals. Lawrence failed to bring Rananim into existence because he did not have the 'blueprint' of the spiritual community. We have the blueprint, but we shall no more be able to bring the spiritual community into existence than he was unless we can become true individuals and can relate to one another as such. Even though we make the effort that this involves, we shall make it all the more successfully if we have even a little of the sensitivity and creativity of the Lawrence who lives so vividly in the pages of Mr Sagar's biography.

Buddhism and William Blake

Buddhism is a universal teaching. It speaks to all men. It speaks to them, moreover, not as belonging to any particular social group, e.g. clan, tribe, caste, race, nation, but as individual human beings. What it tells each one of them is that he can grow — that he can grow from manhood into Buddhahood, or from unenlightened humanity into enlightened humanity. It also tells him how he can do this. When Buddhism speaks to men in this way it of course has to speak to them in a language which they can understand. This means much more than speaking to them in their own vernacular. It means communicating with them through the medium of their own ideas, their own culture. Since Buddhism originated in Ancient India it at first had to speak — the Buddha had to speak — the language of Ancient Indian culture. In fact it had to speak the language of two cultures, the Shramanic and the Brahmanic. Later, when Buddhism spread outside India, it had to speak the language of other cultures, in particular those of South-east Asia, China, Japan, and Tibet. (Sometimes, when the indigenous 'linguistic' resources were inadequate, it had to take Indian culture along with it, but that is another story.) Since Buddhism did not spread beyond Asia, all the cultures with which it came into contact, and through which it had to communicate, were Asian cultures. Although it is in reality a universal teaching, when identified with its medium of communication Buddhism tends to appear as a phenomenon of the cultural history of the East. It tends to appear as an Eastern religion.

During the last century Buddhism has begun to spread beyond Asia. It has begun to make contact with Western culture. As yet, however, it has not really begun to communicate through the medium of that culture. Western Buddhists, and those interested in Buddhism, therefore have to study it in a foreign language, as it were, i.e. through the medium of one or another Asian culture. The situation is made more difficult by the fact that what Asian Buddhist teachers bring to the West is, only too often, not so much Buddhism as the cultural forms with which, for them, it is associated, even identified. Buddhism will not really spread in the West until it speaks the language of Western culture. This will take time. One of the ways in which we can hasten the process is by bringing Buddhism into contact with those Western poets, thinkers, and mystics in whose life or work, or both, there is a reflection, however faint, of the supra-historical splendours of the principial Dharma and who, therefore, already communicate to us something of the spirit of Buddhism in the language of Western culture. One of the greatest of these winged spirits is the English poet, prophet, and visionary William Blake.

Blake was born in London on 28th November 1757, and died there on 12th August 1827. His life thus coincided with one of the most momentous periods in English — indeed in modern Western — history. As a young man he saw and welcomed the American and French Revolutions, while in middle life he was witness to the tremendous upheavals of the Napoleonic wars. He also lived through the Industrial Revolution, with all the changes that this brought about in the social, economic, and political life of the nation. Although he lived in such eventful times,

Blake's outward life at least was uneventful. He attended a drawing school for a few years (the only formal education he received), and when he was fifteen his father, a hosier, apprenticed him to an engraver, with whom he spent the customary seven years learning his trade. Thereafter Blake supported himself by his own labour, but since the skill of the engraver was less in demand than previously he had often to fight a losing battle with poverty and want — a battle that ended only with his death. In 1782 he married the daughter of a market-gardener, and though childless the union was a happy one. From 1782 to 1827 only two events occurred to interrupt the even tenor of Blake's existence in a succession of London lodgings and his work as engraver, poet, painter, and printer of his own illuminated books. The first of these was when, at the invitation of his would-be patron Hayley, he and his wife left London for Felpham, a village on the coast of West Sussex, where they lived — not very happily — for three years (1801-1803). The second occurred shortly after this period of exile when, as a result of an incident with a drunken soldier which had taken place the previous summer, at Felpham, Blake was accused of seditious libel and tried for the capital crime of high treason. Apart from these two events, both of which made a deep impression on him, the history of the greater part of Blake's life is the history of his spiritual realizations and his creative work.

This truer history begins quite early, for Blake's extraordinary qualities quickly revealed themselves. When only four years old he saw God looking in at the window, which set him screaming, and thereafter visionary experiences of this sort were not uncommon. Indeed, they became part of his ordinary waking life. His literary and artistic development was no less rapid. It has been said of him that he 'became an artist at the age of ten, and a poet at the age of twelve'. More remarkable still, his tastes and preferences were very decided, and he showed striking independence of judgement. As he wrote long afterwards, 'I saw and knew immediately the difference between Raffaelle and Rubens'. This was not a difference that was apparent to everybody at the time, but neither then nor in later life did Blake ever hesitate to differ from — or to denounce - even the most respected authorities. Both as a man and as an artist he thought and felt and spoke for himself, without fear and without favour. Independence and originality were in fact among his most outstanding characteristics, together with sturdy self-confidence, honesty, openness and extreme vehemence of expression. But much as his independence and originality contributed to the ultimate greatness of his achievement, they tended to isolate him from his contemporaries. Some people thought him mad. Although he is generally included among the older generation of the romantic poets, along with Wordsworth, Coleridge, and Southey, and his life and work accounted part of the Romantic Movement, his personal contact with them was of the slightest, and they knew hardly anything of his work. Southey, indeed, was among those who thought him mad. Yet despite isolation, and even neglect, Blake's life was a happy one, and towards the end of it he had the satisfaction of gathering around him a small group of young artists who loved and venerated him. When death came he was ready. 'His countenance became fair, his eyes brightened, and he burst out singing.'

Being so much an individual himself, it was only natural that Blake should uphold the importance of the general principle of individuality. Indeed, he regarded it as the indispensable basis of true morality and true religion. For him the individual was sacred and inviolable. He therefore believed that it was the duty of each man to be himself, to develop his own potentialities to the utmost, and to allow others to do likewise. 'The Worship of God,' he wrote in one of his finest passages, 'is honouring his gifts in other men; & loving the greatest men best, each according to his Genius: which is the Holy Ghost in man'. Blake meant this quite literally: for him God is man, and there is no other God. In another passage he insists that vice is not so much giving expression to one's own energies as hindering the energies of others. Man cannot develop his potentialities unless he is free. The corollary of the principle of individuality is the principle of liberty. As a young man Blake was a revolutionary, and he therefore saw liberty in primarily social and political terms, as freedom from the tyranny of kings and priests. Later his ideas changed, or rather they developed as he developed, and he saw it first psychologically, as the liberation of the instinctual and emotional energies from the bondage of reason, and then as the liberation of the whole man from the internal divisions into which he had fallen, including the division between reason and emotion. True liberty was to exercise 'the Divine Arts of Imagination'. It was to expand one's consciousness, exploring 'inward into the Worlds of Thought'. It was to enter, or rather re-enter, Eternity.

Blake's enlarged conception of liberty corresponds to an enlarged conception of man. Man is not twofold but fourfold, consisting of the body and its instincts, reason, the emotions, and imagination. This obviously anticipates Jung's four basic functions of sensation, thought, feeling, and intuition. There is also some resemblance to the first four of the five Spiritual Faculties of Buddhist tradition, i.e. to (in matching order) Vigour (*virya*), Wisdom (*prajñā*), faith and devotion (*shraddhā*), and concentration (*samādhi*), although the fact that these are accompanied by a fifth spiritual faculty, that of Mindfulness (*smriti*), which balances Faith and Wisdom, and Vigour and Concentration, means that all four are raised to a higher level and enabled to work together for the attainment of Enlightenment. For Blake man is fourfold both in his divided and in his undivided state. In his fallen and divided state the body and its instincts are present as his Shadow, by which Blake meant suppressed desires, the emotions as his (fallen) Emanation, or split-off feminine counterpart, while reason is present as his Spectre, which is also the self-centred Selfhood with which the fallen man now identifies himself. Imagination, or his Humanity, is absent, or rather is in abeyance, sunk 'in deadly sleep'. Within the context of this enlarged conception of man the individual develops his potentialities when his Humanity awakes. When his Humanity awakes, i.e. when he identifies himself with his Imagination, he can enter his Shadow, absorb his Emanation, and cast out (and also love) his Spectre. In man's unfallen and undivided state, or in Eternity, the four basic functions appear in their 'archetypal' forms as what Blake calls the Four Zoas.

These are Tharmas, 'the mildest son of heaven', the Zoa of sense; Urizen, the Prince of Light, the Zoa of reason; Luvah, the Prince of Love, the Zoa of the emotions; and Urthona, 'the keeper of the gates of heaven', the Zoa of Imagination. There is thus a correspondence, in the hermetic sense, not only between the four basic functions and the Four Zoas, but also between Shadow, (fallen) Emanation, Spectre, and sleeping Humanity and the Four Zoas, in other words between the fallen and divided and the unfallen and undivided states of the four basic functions. This is not unlike the general correspondence, in the Mahayana and Vajrayana forms of Buddhism, between Samsāra and Nirvana, kleśa (defilement), and bodhi (Enlightenment), or, more specifically, between the five poisons of delusion, hatred, pride, craving, and jealousy, and the mandala of the Five Jinas or Five Buddhas, i.e. (in matching order), Vairochana, Akshobhya,

Ratnasambhava, Amitabha, and Amoghasiddhi. There is, however, one important difference. In Buddhism there is no doctrine concerning the absolute beginning of things, which is said to be imperceptible. Saṁsāra does not originate from Nirvana; bodhi never becomes the *kleśas*. In Blake's system the Four Zoas divide one from another and fall from Eternity into time, from Truth into error. They fall in anticlockwise order. Tharmas, whose compass point is west, enters time first, followed by Urizen (south), Luvah (east), and Urthona (north). The story of how the Zoas fell, and what terrible conflicts took place between them and their Emanations, as well as the story of how they were all delivered and restored to unity, constitutes Blake's great myth. It is this myth which, in various stages of development, forms the subject matter of the major 'prophetic books', especially the second longest of them, the central but unfinished *Vala*, or *The Four Zoas*.

The correspondence between psychic functions and Zoas, and poisons and Buddhas, is not the only one. Both Blake and Vajrayana Buddhism see the whole of existence as one vast and complex system of correspondences. Both use the hermetic principle, as it may be termed, as a principle of order, as a means of organizing the more prominent features of our experience into a beautiful and meaningful pattern, i.e. into a mandala, and in this way achieve integration. Both Blake and Vajrayana Buddhism are therefore concerned to establish sets of correlations, some of them natural and obvious, others apparently quite arbitrary. Blake correlates the Four Zoas not only with the four basic psychic functions, but also with various other sets of four, such as the four points of the compass, the four worlds, the four occupations, the four metals, the four continents, the four arts, the four quarters of the British Isles, the four cities, and the four senses. Thus Tharmas, the Zoa of sense, is associated with the western direction, the world of generation, the occupation of shepherd, the metal brass, the continent of America, the art of painting, Ireland, the city of York, and the tongue or sense of taste. Some of the correlations are quite elaborate (though not without minor discrepancies), such as those between the counties of Great Britain and the Sons of Israel, and the counties of England and the Sons of Albion. Blake's system of correspondences is most fully worked out in *Jerusalem, the Emanation of the Giant Albion*, the longest of the prophetic books, and the last. In much the same way Vajrayana Buddhism correlates the Five Jinas or Five Buddhas not only with the five poisons but with the five wisdoms (*jñānas*), the five colours, the five directions, the five elements, the five mudras or hand-gestures, the five emblems, the five vehicles or mounts, and the five 'aggregates' (*skandhas*). (The Vajrayana deals in pentads rather than tetrads inasmuch as the 'central' Buddha Vairochana and his 'absolute' wisdom represent the unity of the other four — though according to an early Buddhist Tantric tradition 'everything goes in fours'.) Thus the Buddha Akshobhya, the 'Imperturbable', is associated with the mirror-like wisdom, the colour blue, the eastern direction, the element water, the earth-touching mudra, the emblem of the vajra or 'mystic thunderbolt', the elephant vehicle, and the aggregate of form (*rūpa*). There are, of course, many other sets of correlations. Both Blake and Vajrayana Buddhism see a correspondence between the order in which the Four Zoas, or the Four Buddhas (i.e. the Five Buddhas minus Vairochana, the Buddha of the centre) are distributed round the four quarters of the mandala and the successive stages by which the individual develops his potentialities. Beginning with Tharmas in the west, the Four Zoas enter into time in anticlockwise order, which is the order in which their corresponding psychic functions develop in the individual. In Buddhism, of course, there is no original cosmic fall, but when the Four Buddhas, beginning with Amoghasiddhi in the north, are enumerated in anticlockwise order this corresponds to the order in which, upon the occurrence of the profound spiritual experience of 'turning about' (*parāvritti*), the five sense-consciousnesses, the mind-consciousness, the soiled-mind-consciousness, and the (relative) store-consciousness, are transformed into the corresponding four Buddha-wisdoms. It also corresponds to the *clockwise* order in which the Five Buddhas appear to the consciousness of the deceased person in 'The Tibetan Book of the Dead' (where, so far as the individual is concerned, a 'fall' may indeed occur), as well as to the order in which they are depicted as constituent parts of the visualized seed-syllable HUṀ in the Yoga of the Long HUṀ.

Blake's emphasis on the importance of individuality connects not only with his conception of man and his system of correspondences but also with his deep insight into the true nature of the individual. Man is in reality not a natural but a spiritual being, and his essence is eternal. Nature has, indeed, no existence apart from man, and like man is fundamentally spiritual, being simply 'a portion of soul [i.e. the emotions] discerned by the five senses, the chief inlets of soul in this age'. Nature appears as a separate entity from man only after the fall, when the individual's senses are turned inside out, so that he perceives what is internal as external, and when, forgetting his true existence, he passes through various states or worlds. These states are quite different from the individual who passes through them, and it is important that the two should be distinguished. States can change, and be annihilated, but individuals cannot. States may be judged and condemned, but individuals can only be forgiven. This is Blake's great doctrine of the Forgiveness of Sins, and since the Forgiveness of Sins is mutual it is the basis of the

Brotherhood of Man. The way in which fallen man passes, like a traveller, through various states or worlds, is not unlike the way in which, according to Buddhist tradition, the ever-changing stream of consciousness wanders as a result of spiritual ignorance (*āvidyā*) from one to another of the five (or six) realms of conditioned existence, appearing now as a god, now as an animal, and now as a man, and so on, through a whole series of lives until, with the cessation of craving and the attainment of Nirvana, the process of compulsory rebirth comes to an end. In keeping with its refusal to recognize a causal nexus between phenomenal existence and the Absolute, Buddhism does not, of course, speak of a fallen Buddha who wanders through the five (or six) realms of conditioned existence for a while and then gains, or regains, Enlightenment. Yet there is a parallel between Blake and Buddhism at least so far as the origin of the states or worlds is concerned. According to Blake the states are created by the imagination, or by Jesus (for him it amounts to the same thing), as a means of defining the errors into which man has fallen and thus delivering him from them. In Buddhism, at least in its Tibetan form, Shinje, the Lord of the Dead, who judges people after their death and assigns them a place in the other world according with their deeds, is in reality a form of Avalokiteshvara, the Bodhisattva of Compassion.

The fact that the states are created by the imagination makes it clear that, as Blake insists, 'The Imagination is not a State: it is the Human Existence itself . . .' Since the imagination is also identified with Jesus, and since Jesus is God, the true man is not only the imagination, or poetic genius, but also God. Blake in fact explicitly equates God and man. 'Thou art a Man, God is no more, / Thy own humanity learn to adore . . .' This does not mean that man in his fallen state, or man as a purely animal and rational being, can be set up in the place formerly occupied by

God, as so often happens in the case of secular humanism. It means that instead of submitting to the arbitrary commands of an angry God who dwells high above him in an external heaven man should develop his own imagination, his own Divine Humanity, and become what, in the depths of his being, he truly is. Blake's humanism is a spiritual humanism, and as such is akin to the transcendental humanism of Buddhism, which acknowledges no form of existence higher than a Buddha or perfectly enlightened human being. Blake not only equates God and man but also, with equal explicitness, rejects deism. His position is, in fact, not just non-deistic but even, in effect, non-theistic, and so to that extent not really Christian, at least not in the traditional sense of that term. His name for the 'angry God' is Nobodaddy (i.e. 'nobody's daddy'), and he identifies him with the jealous God of the Old Testament, with Satan the Accuser, and with the fallen Urizen. It is this false God, the God of this world, that is worshipped by the worldly. Blake's position here is broadly that of Gnosticism. He also rejects the religion of this God, which is that of punishment for sin, as well as the dogmas of the Virgin Birth, the Vicarious Atonement, a personal Devil, and an everlasting hell. He rejects, in fact, the whole structure of 'orthodox' Christian belief, and although he considers himself a Christian his version of Christianity — if it can be called that — is not only different from, but diametrically opposed to, the more popular 'Urizenic' version. Blake is fully aware of this opposition. In a well known couplet he declares, 'The vision of Christ that thou dost see, / Is my vision's greatest enemy.' At times he seems to reject not just 'orthodox' Christianity but religion itself, as when he speaks of Jesus sending his seventy-two disciples 'Against religion and government'. One modern commentator in fact says that Blake often used 'religion' as a smear word, and it is true that at his best and most characteristic he speaks in terms of artistic inspiration rather then in terms of religious belief. Even when he does use the language of belief he uses it in his own way, i.e. not literally and dogmatically but metaphorically and symbolically. According to him this is in fact the right way to use it, for all religion is 'decayed poetry' and to understand it poetically is to understand it as it was originally meant to be understood. Then as now, it is the poetic genius, the man of imagination, who is the truly religious man.

A whole century before Buddhism was really known in the West Blake offers us the unique example of a non-theistic imaginative vision of rare intensity and integrity. That he could do this was due in the first place to his own extraordinary creative powers — powers which manifested early, and of which he remained in unimpaired possession to the end of his days, he being faithful to them, and they being faithful to him. It was also due to the fact that in addition to the Bible and the major English poets Chaucer, Spenser, Shakespeare, and Milton (and, of course, the works of Michelangelo and the monuments in Westminster Abbey) Blake was able to draw inspiration — indeed, to derive certain elements of his own system — from the 'alternative tradition' of Agrippa and Paracelsus, Boehme and Swedenborg. He was also indebted to some of his more unorthodox contemporaries, such as the freethinker and radical Thomas Paine, the Swiss poet and theologian Gaspar Lavater, Thomas Taylor 'the Platonist', and the mythologogue William Stukeley. But important though all these were for his development, Blake's combative and fiery genius probably owed as much to his spiritual enemies as to his spiritual friends, for it was largely in opposition to their mistaken beliefs that he formulated his own system. The most distinguished and influential of these enemies — the enemies of Blake's

'Divine Vision' — were Bacon, Newton, and Locke, whose mechanistic science, mechanistic natural philosophy, and mechanistic psychology left no room for imaginative truth or spiritual values. In setting himself in opposition to them — a David against three Goliaths — Blake set himself against the master-current of the age, and in this lies the true measure of his greatness. Indeed, through his life and his creative work Blake accomplishes in his own person what he calls a Last Judgement, which is not a condemnation of sinners to everlasting hell-fire but a final casting out of error from the bosom of the Eternal Man or the imagination. What Blake therefore offers us is not only a non-theistic imaginative vision, — not only something of the spirit of Buddhism in the language of Western culture, — but an example of the kind of radical revaluation of Western religion and culture that Buddhism, in the person of the Western Buddhist, may soon be called upon to undertake.